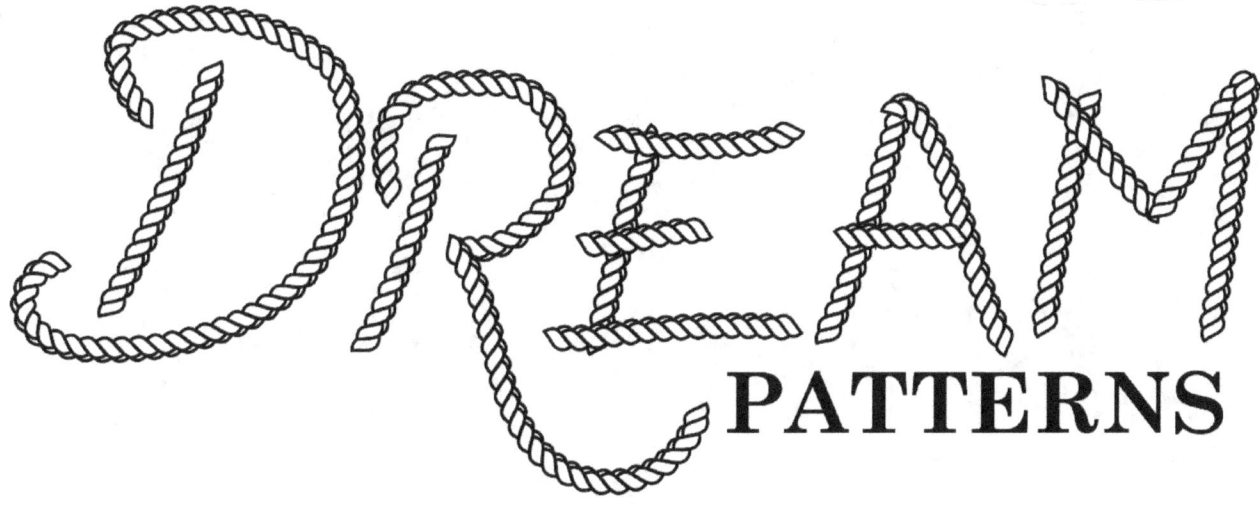

PATTERNS

ADULT COLORING BOOK FOR STRESS RELIEF

Copyright © 2016 Edin S.

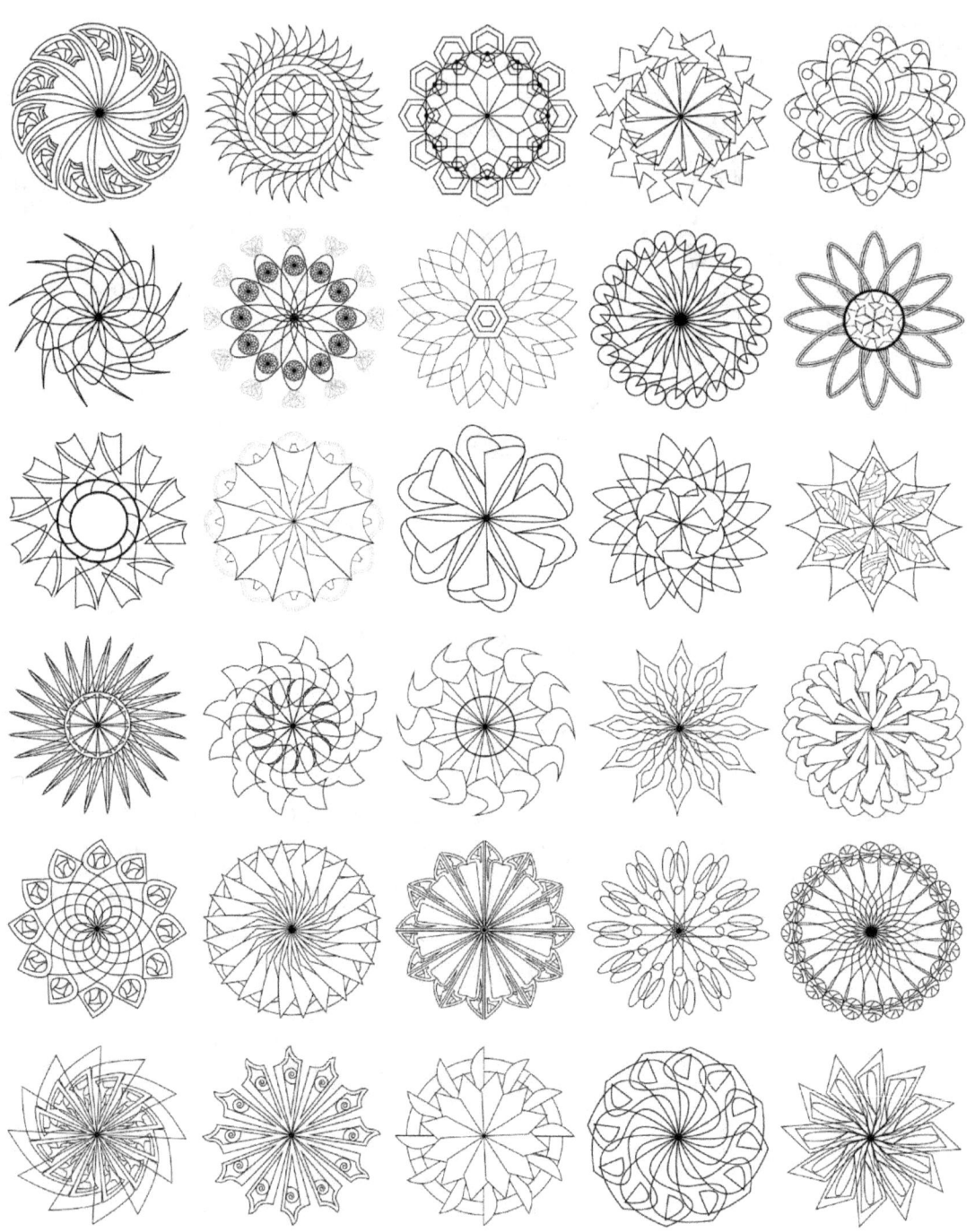

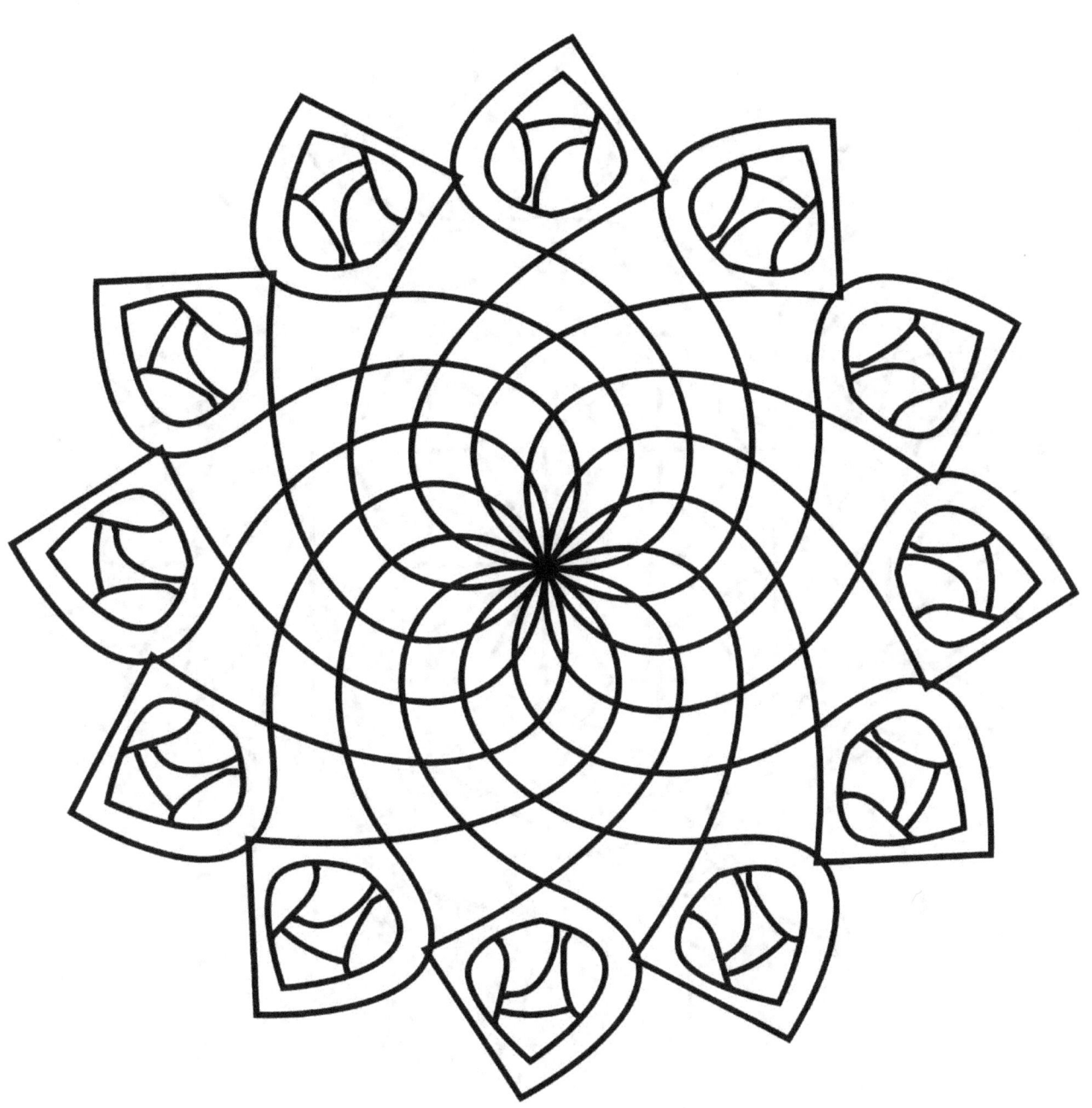

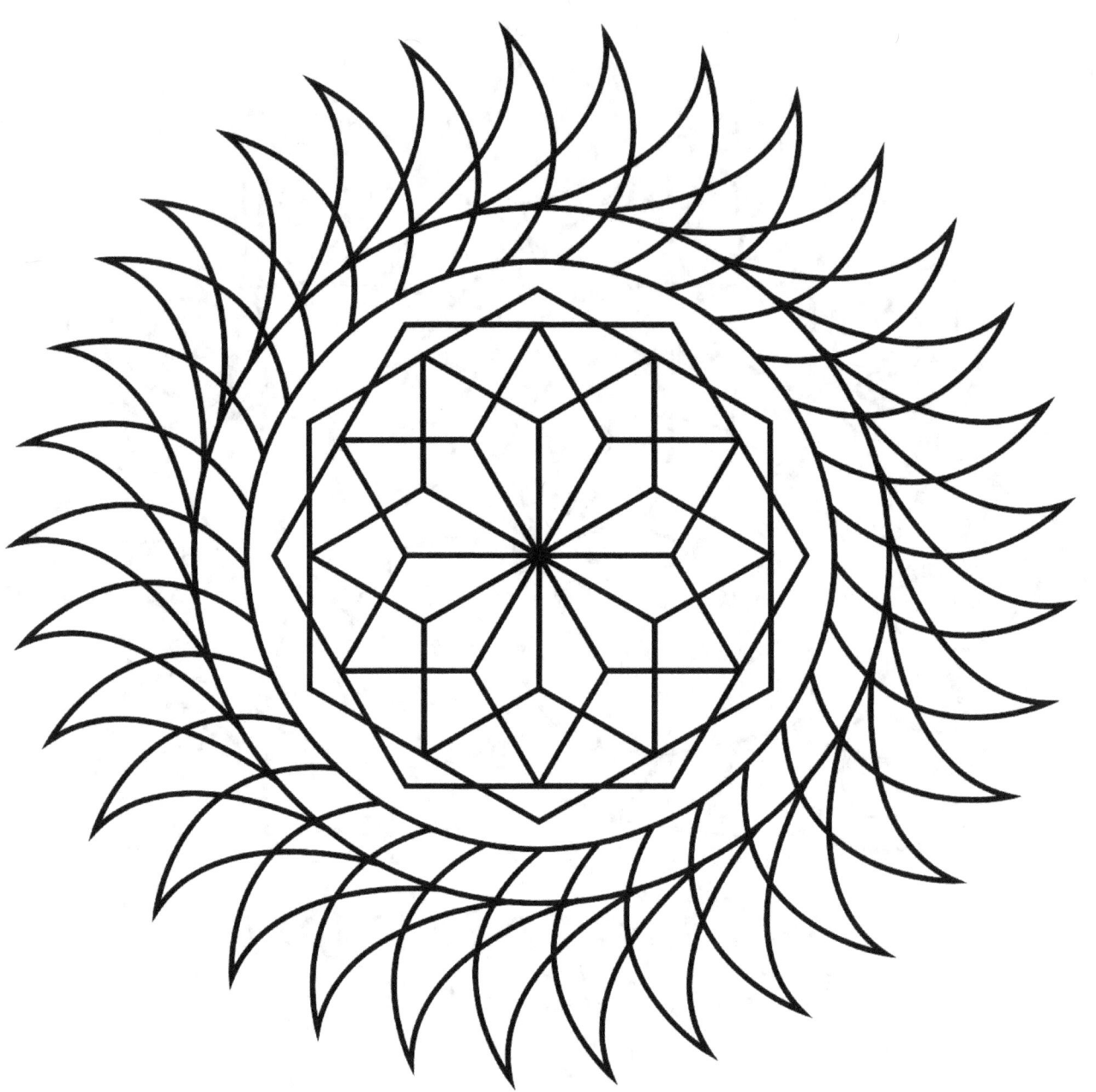

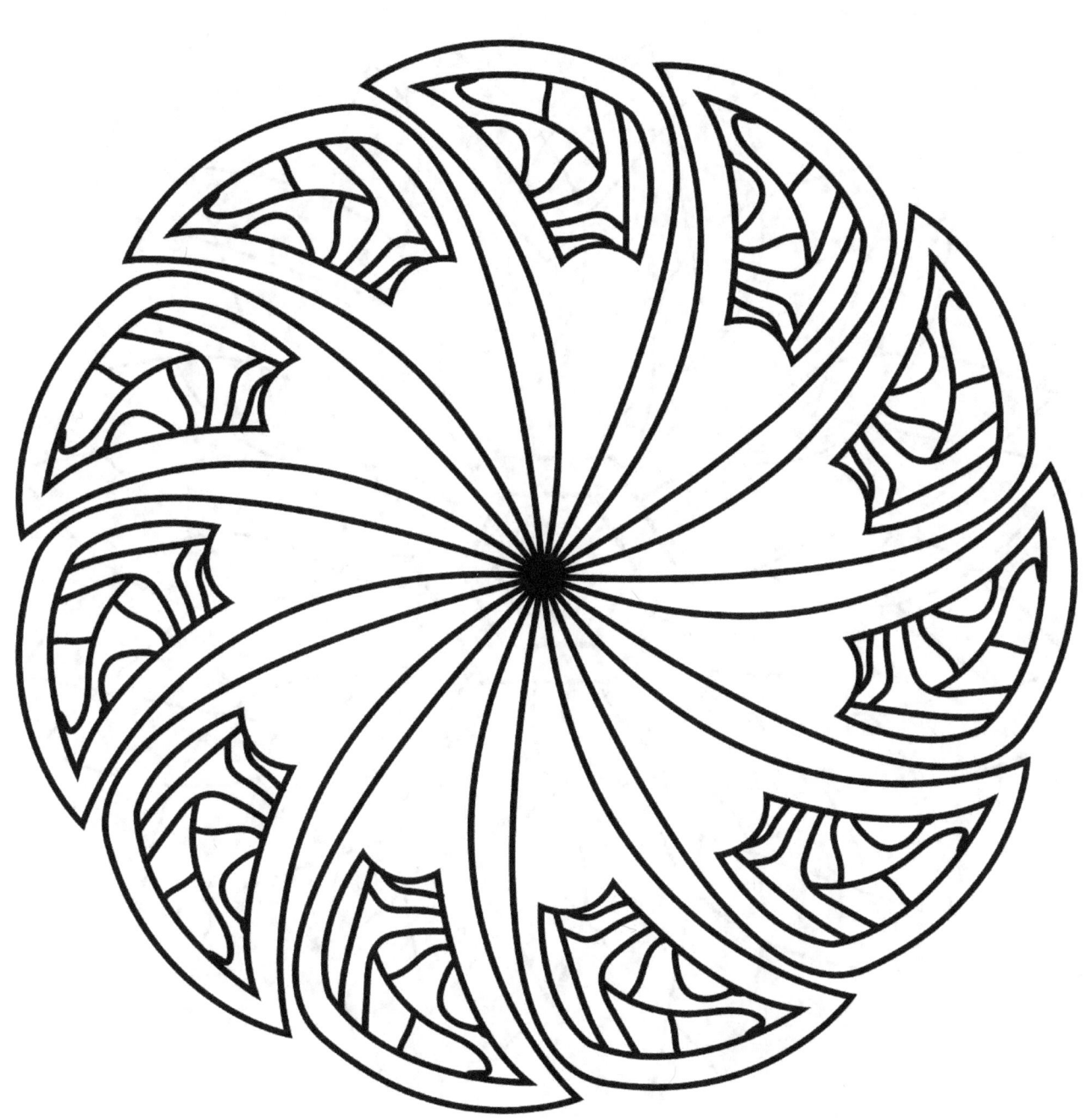

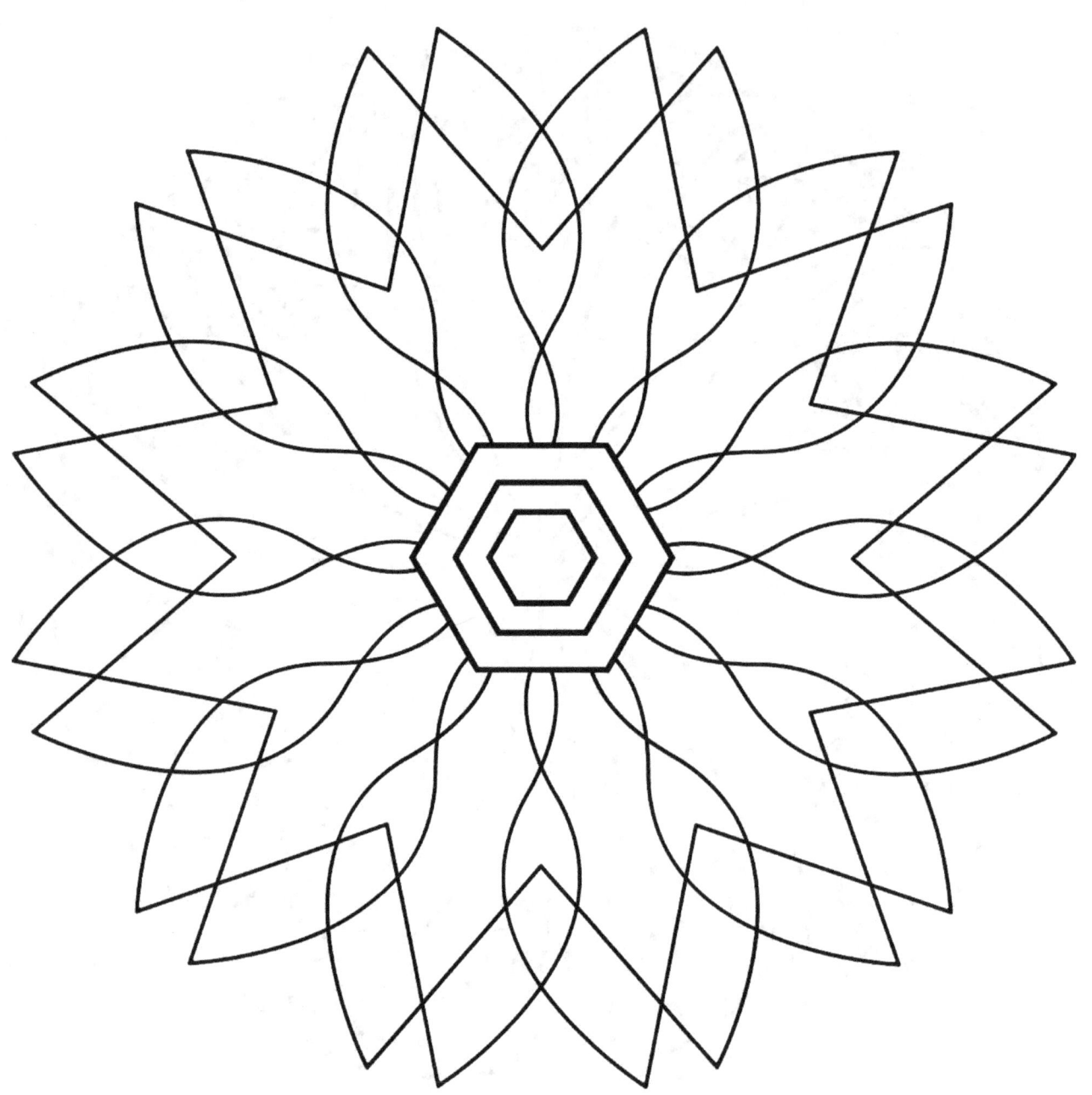

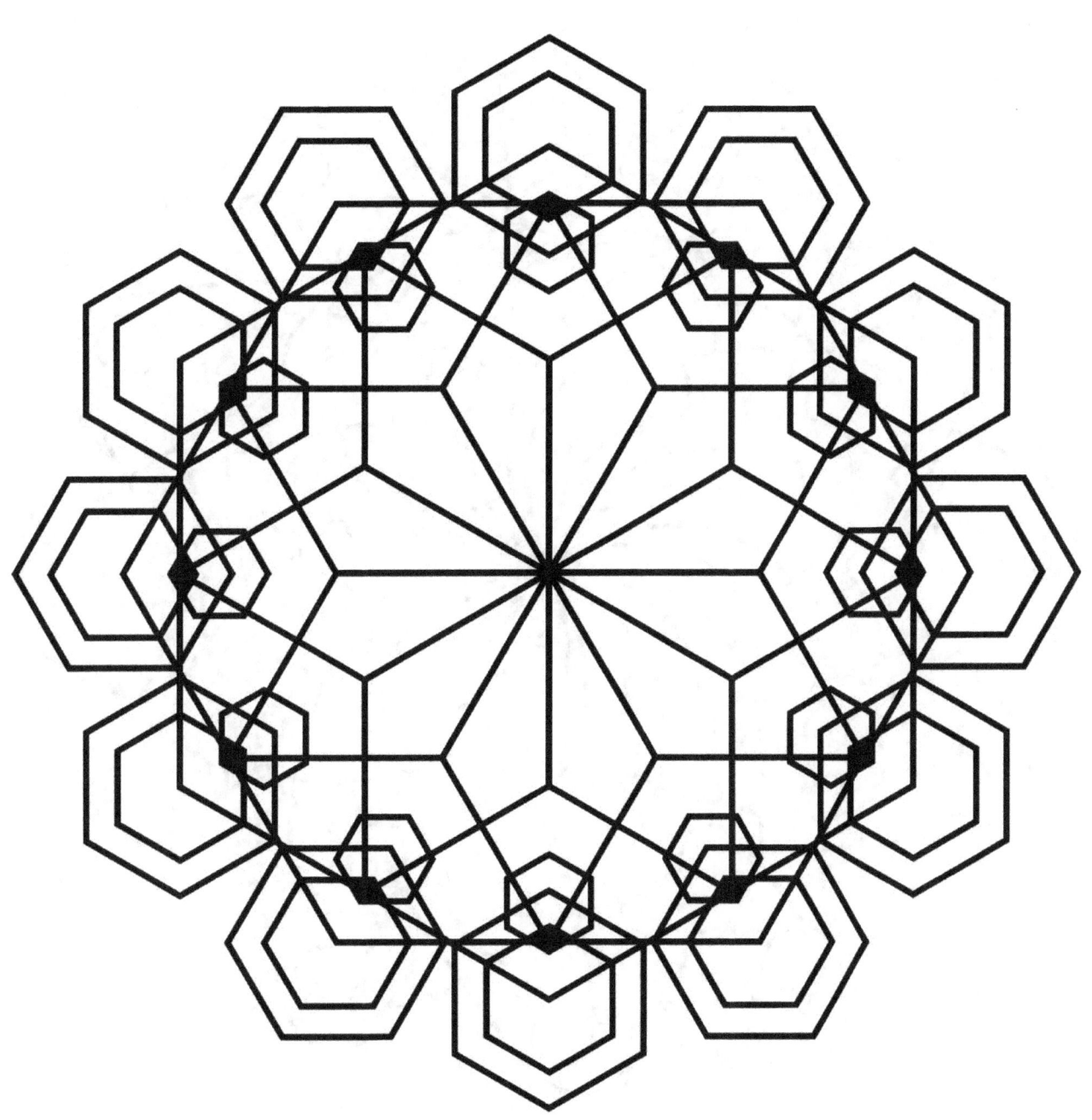

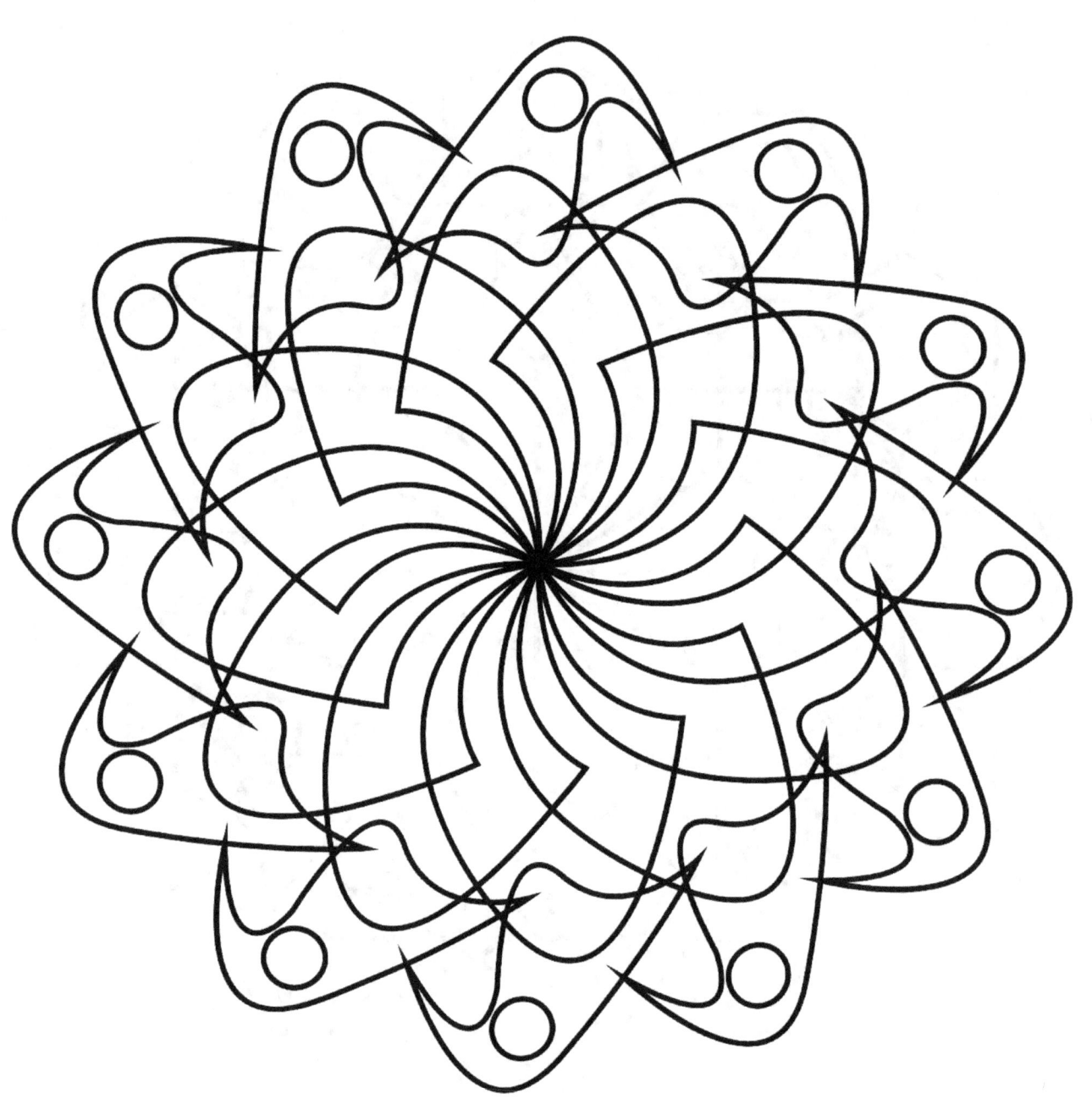

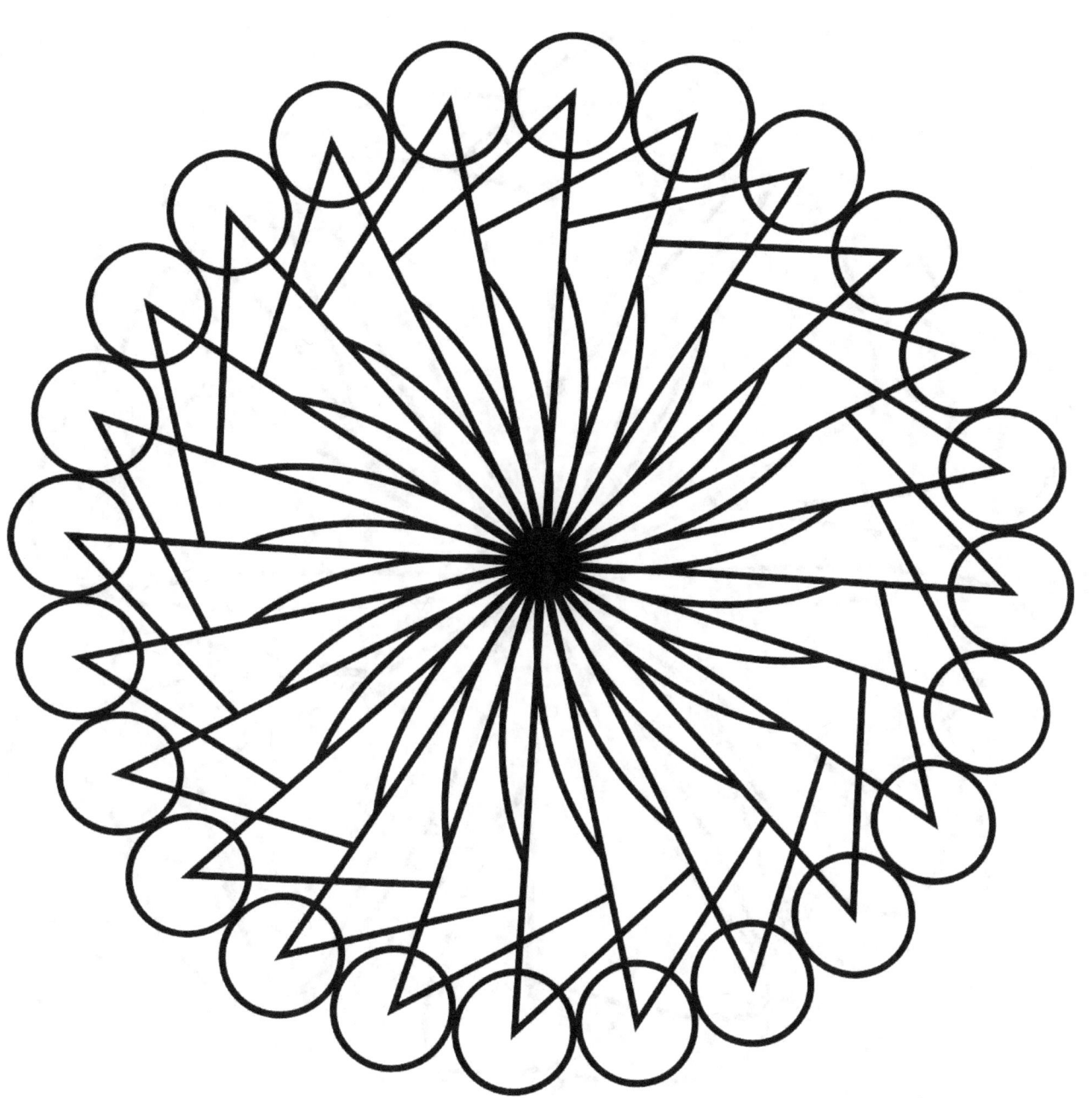

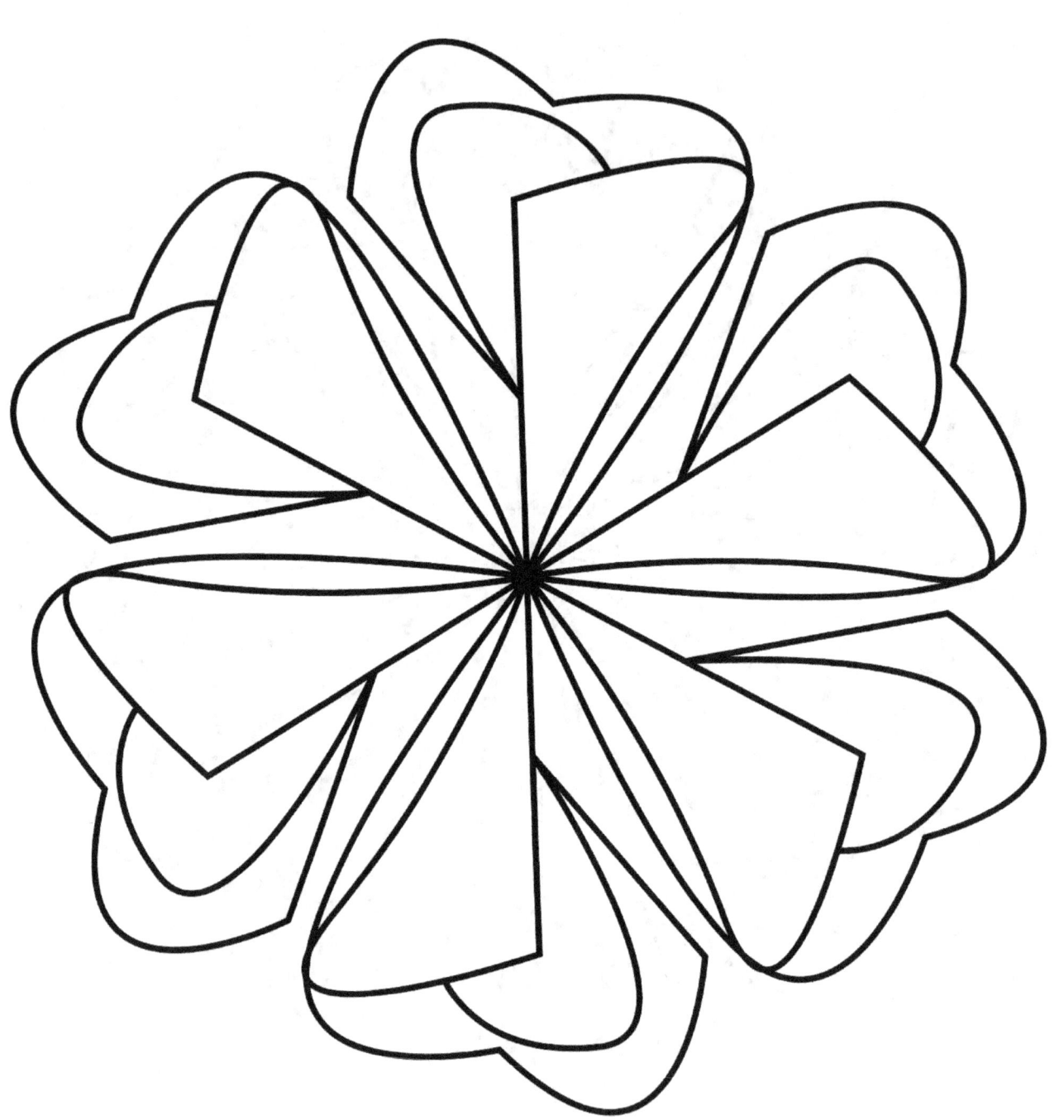

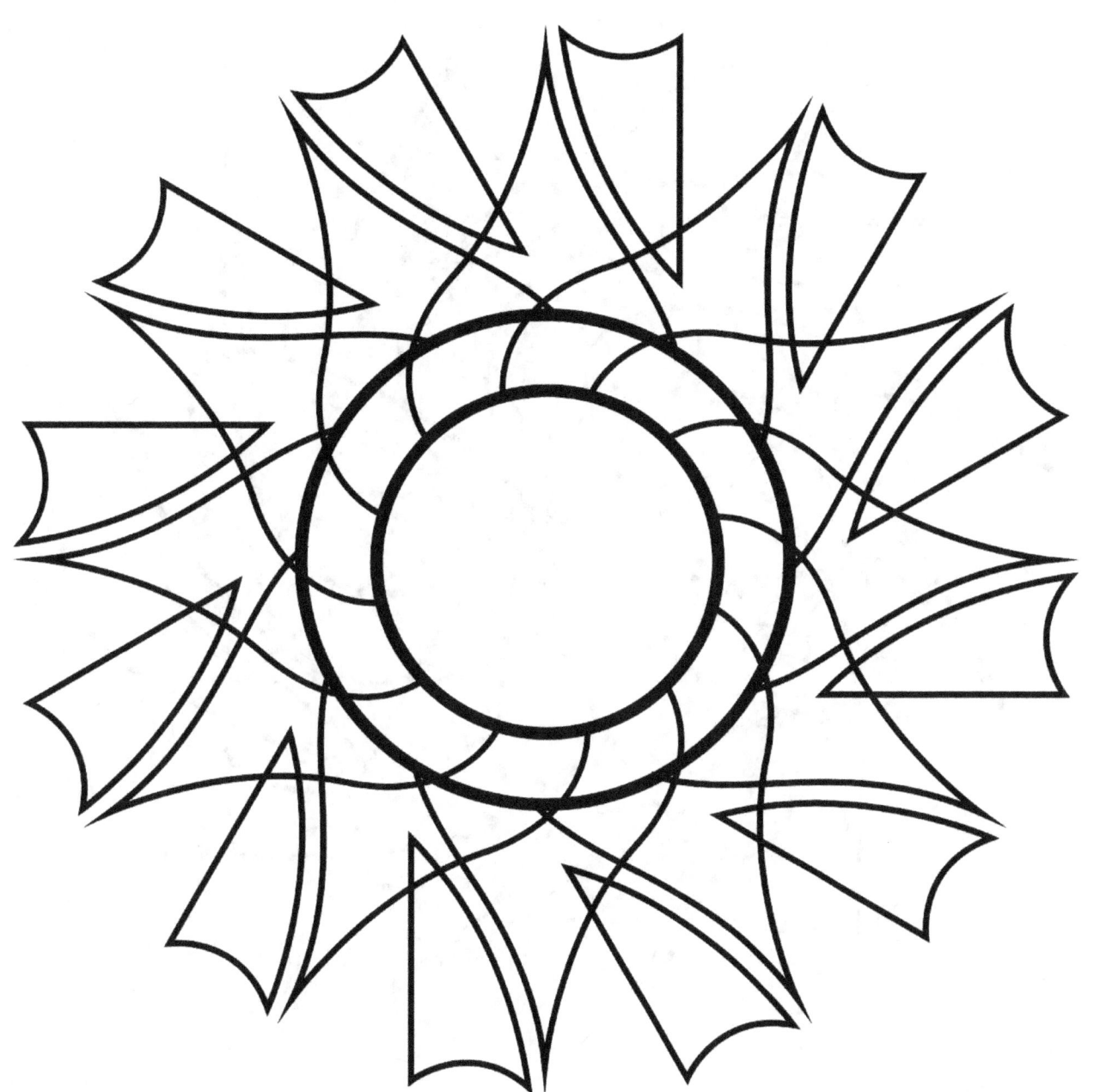

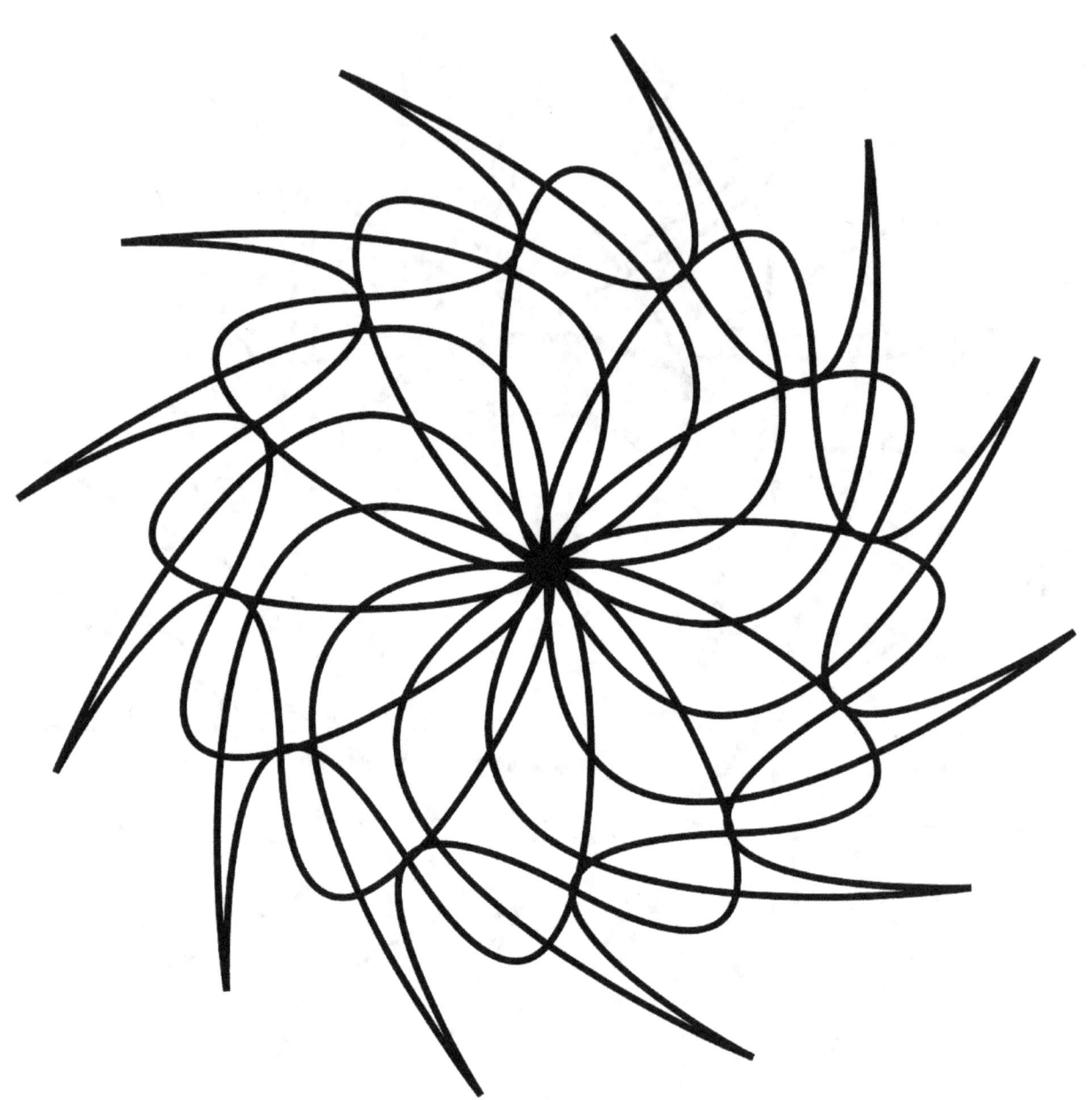

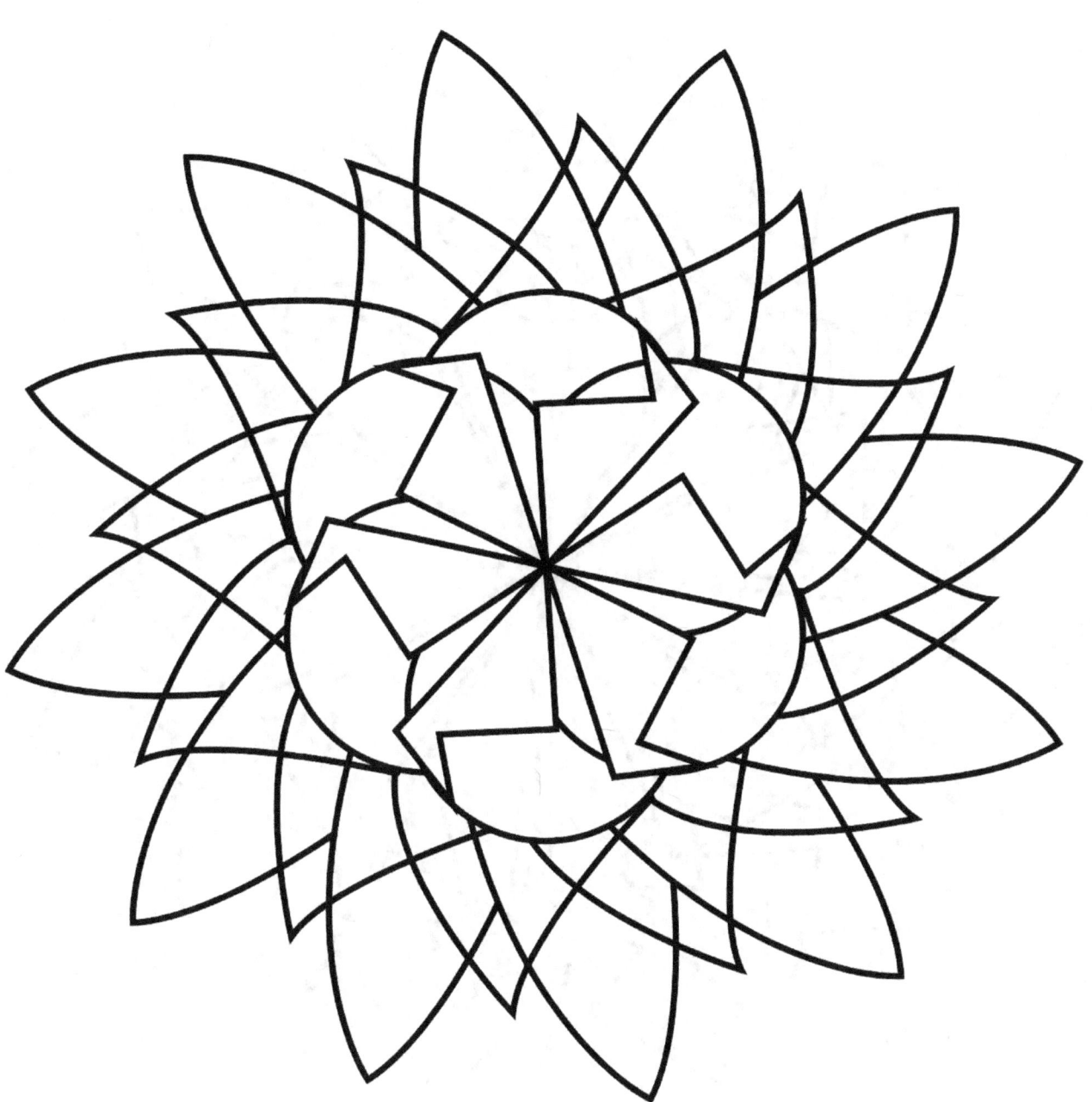

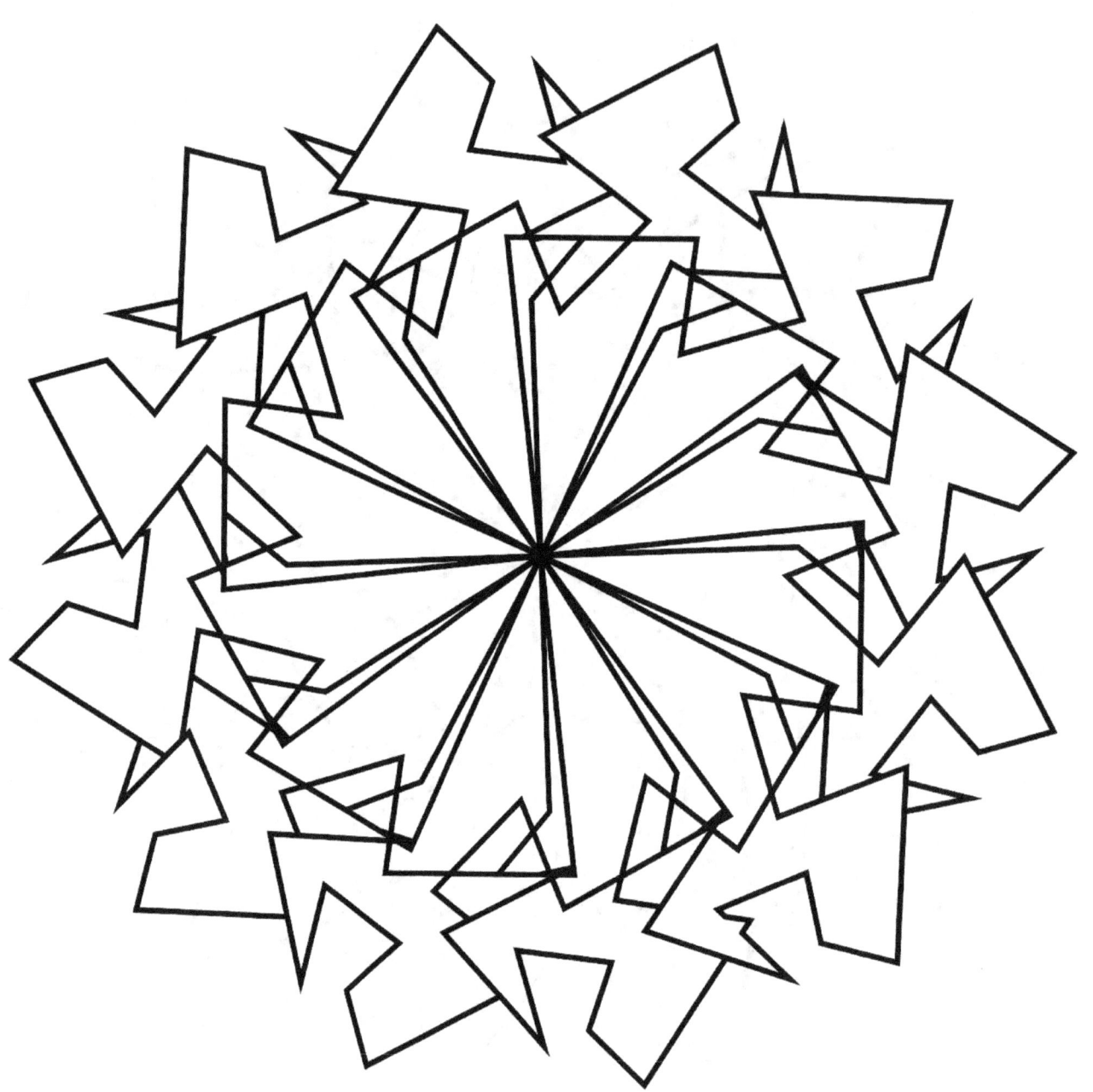

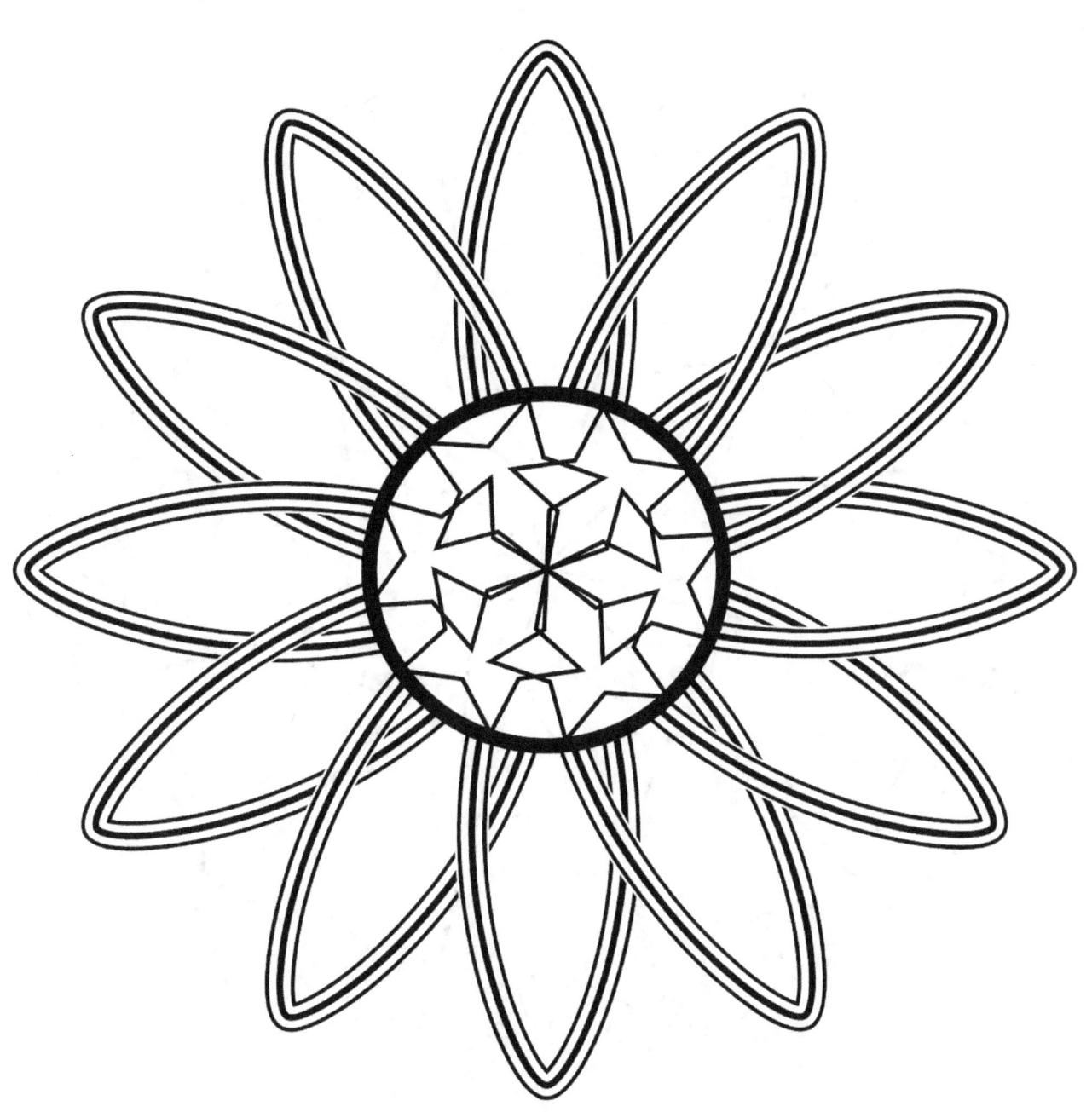

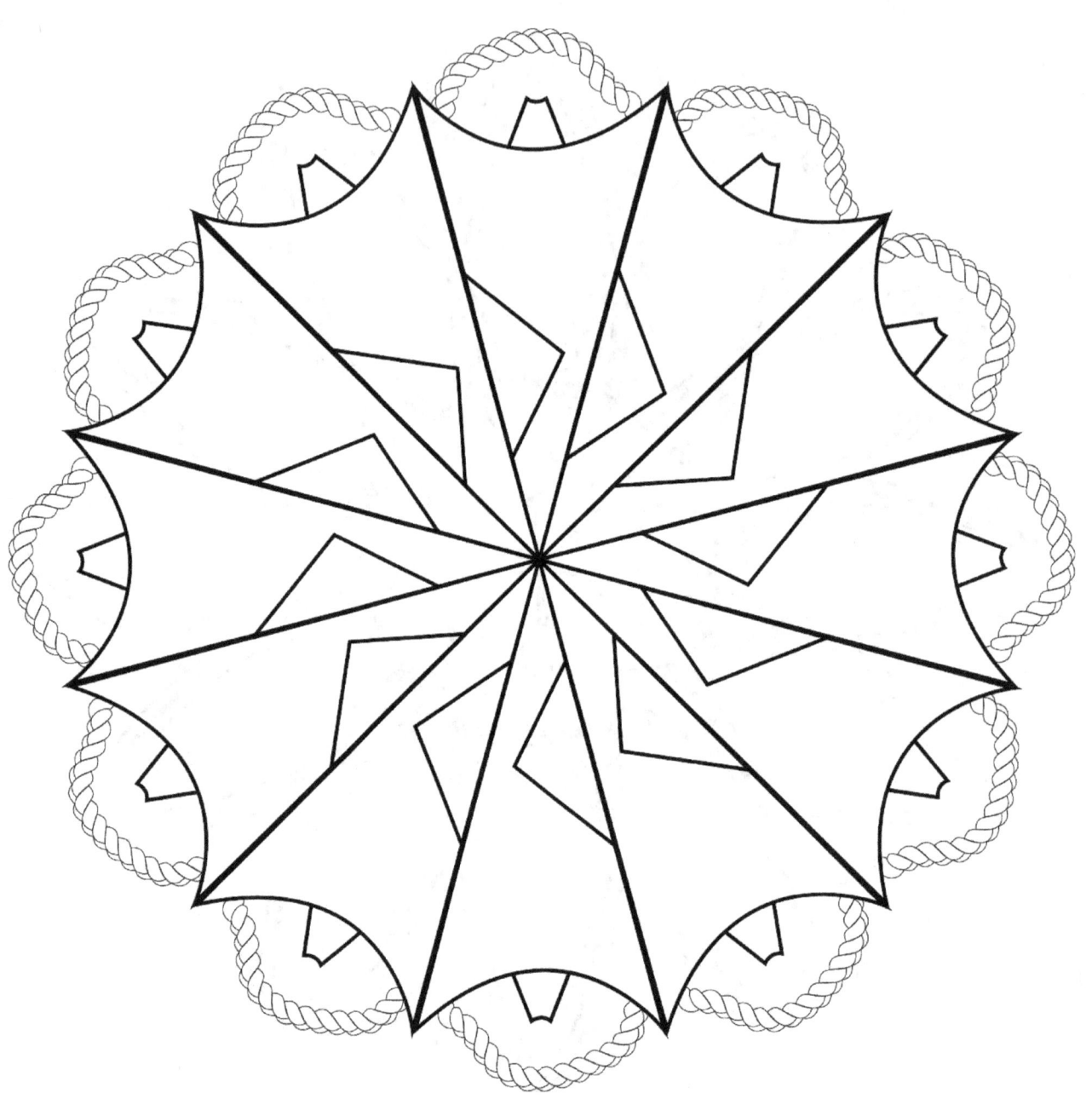

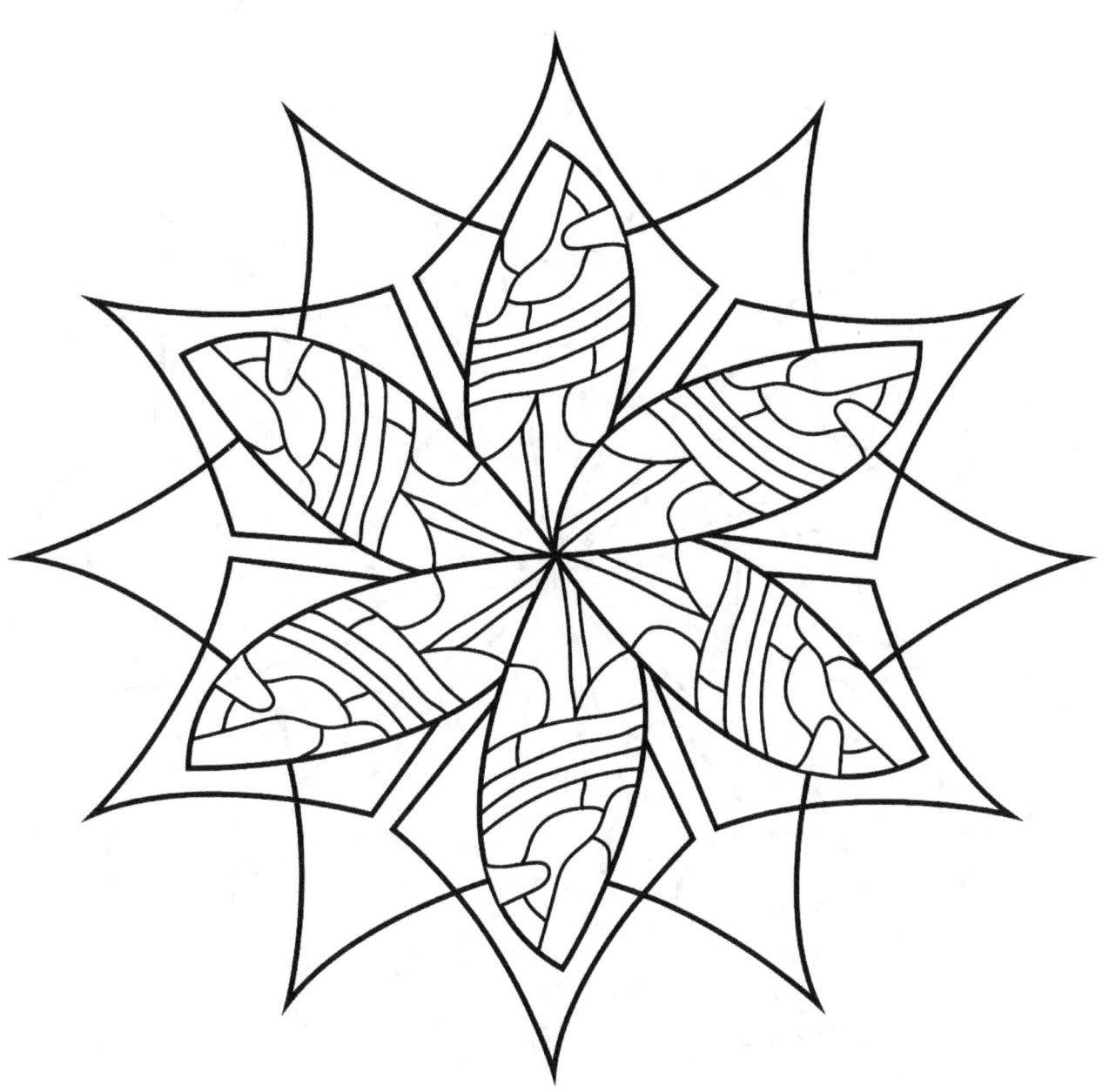

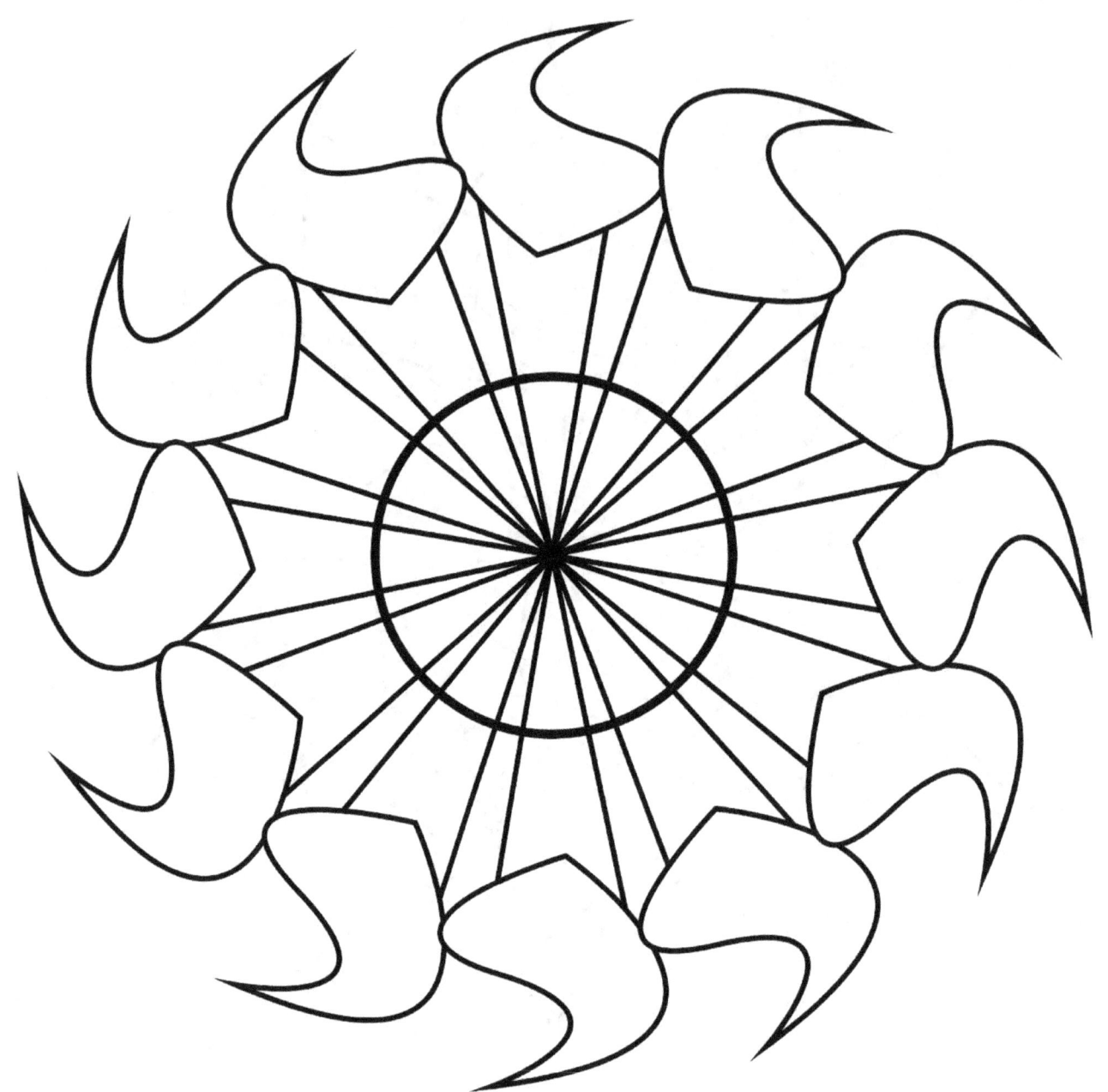

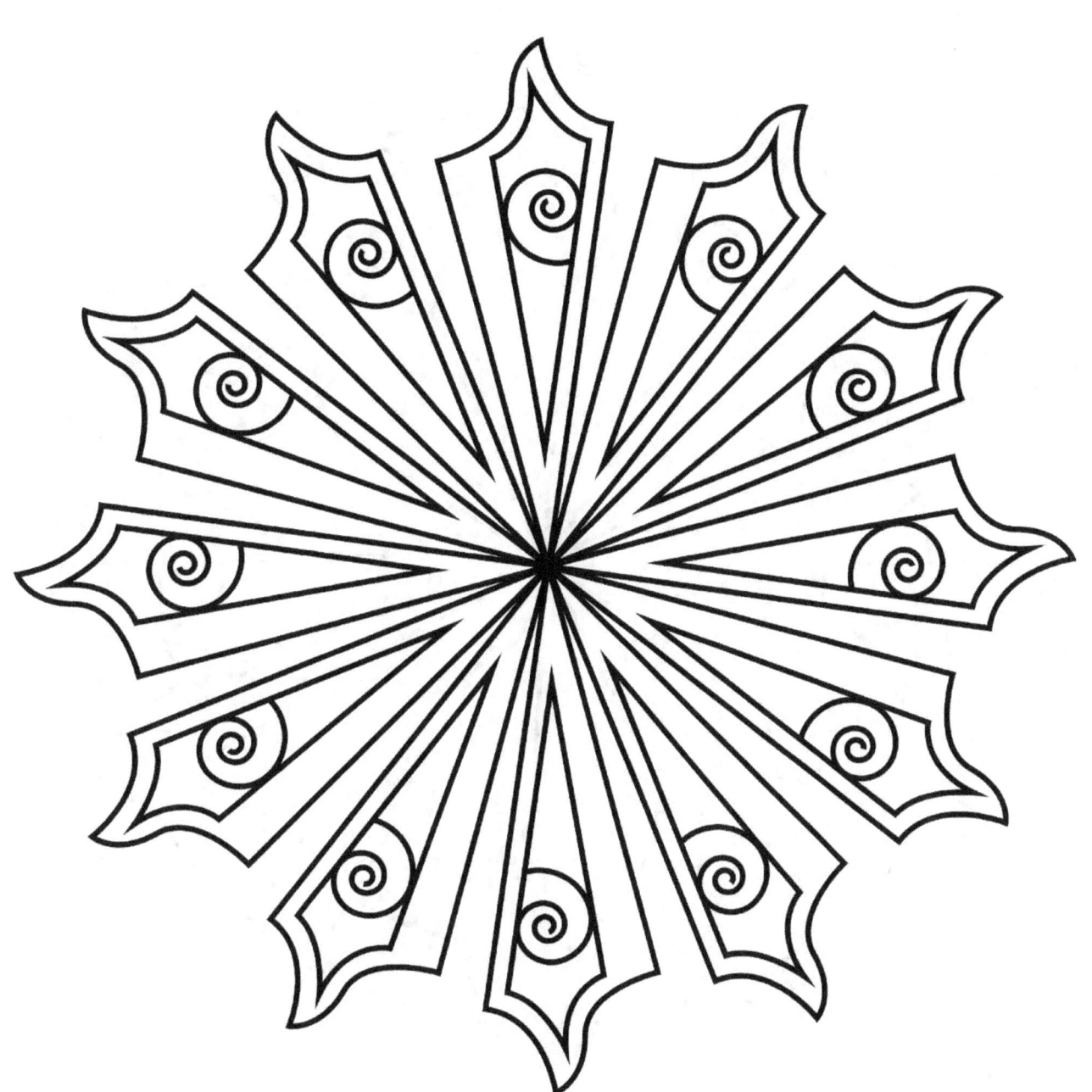

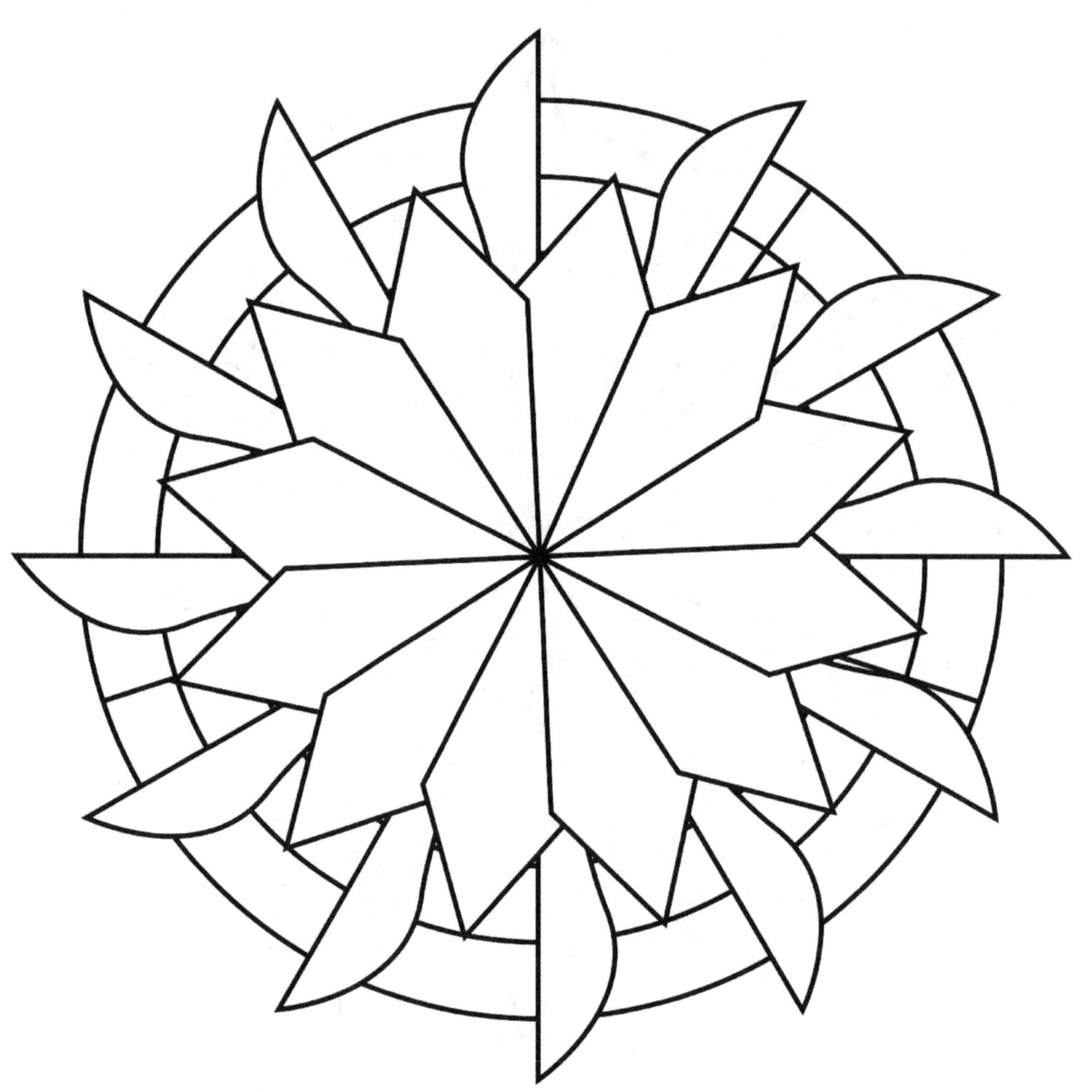

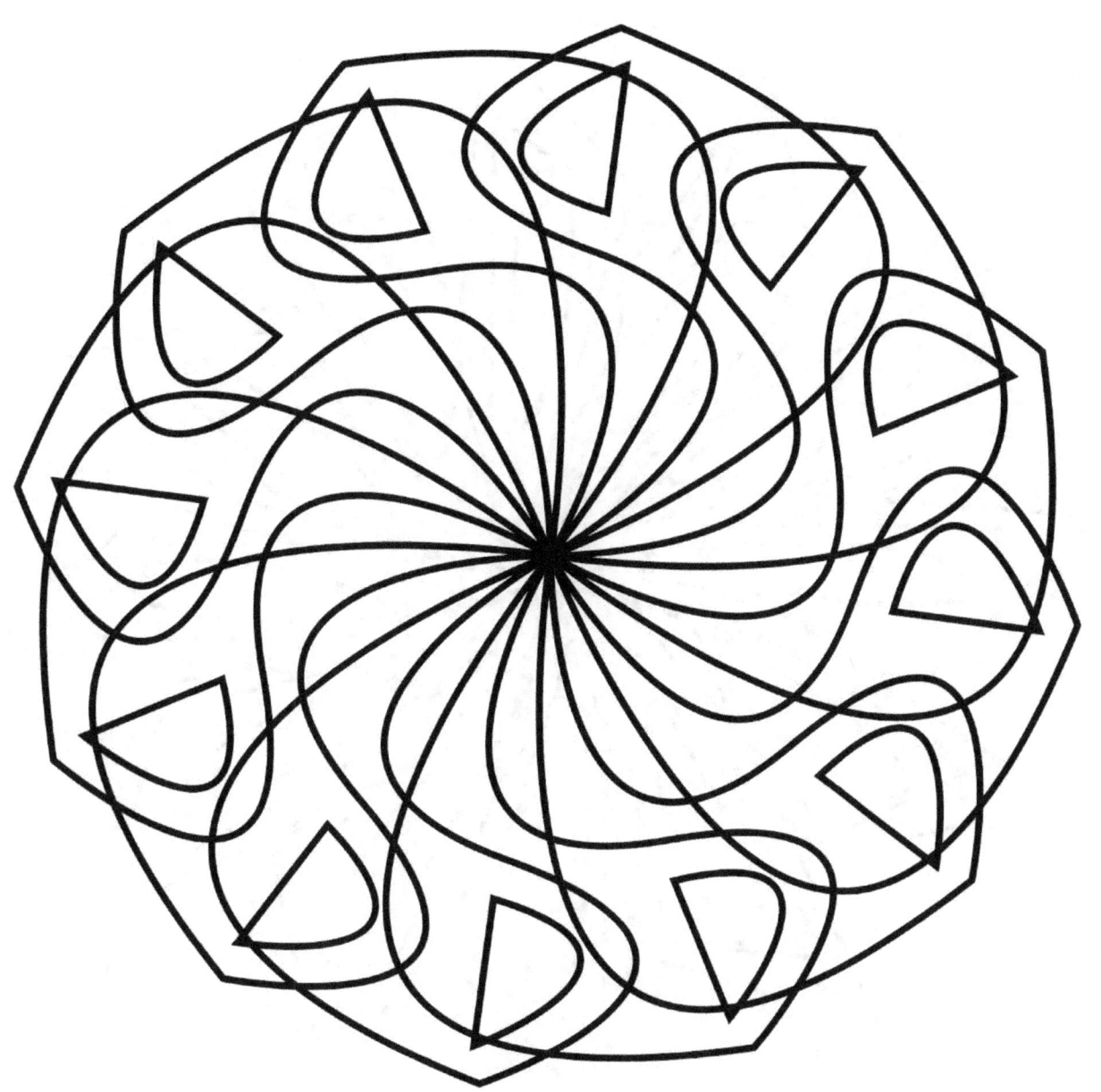

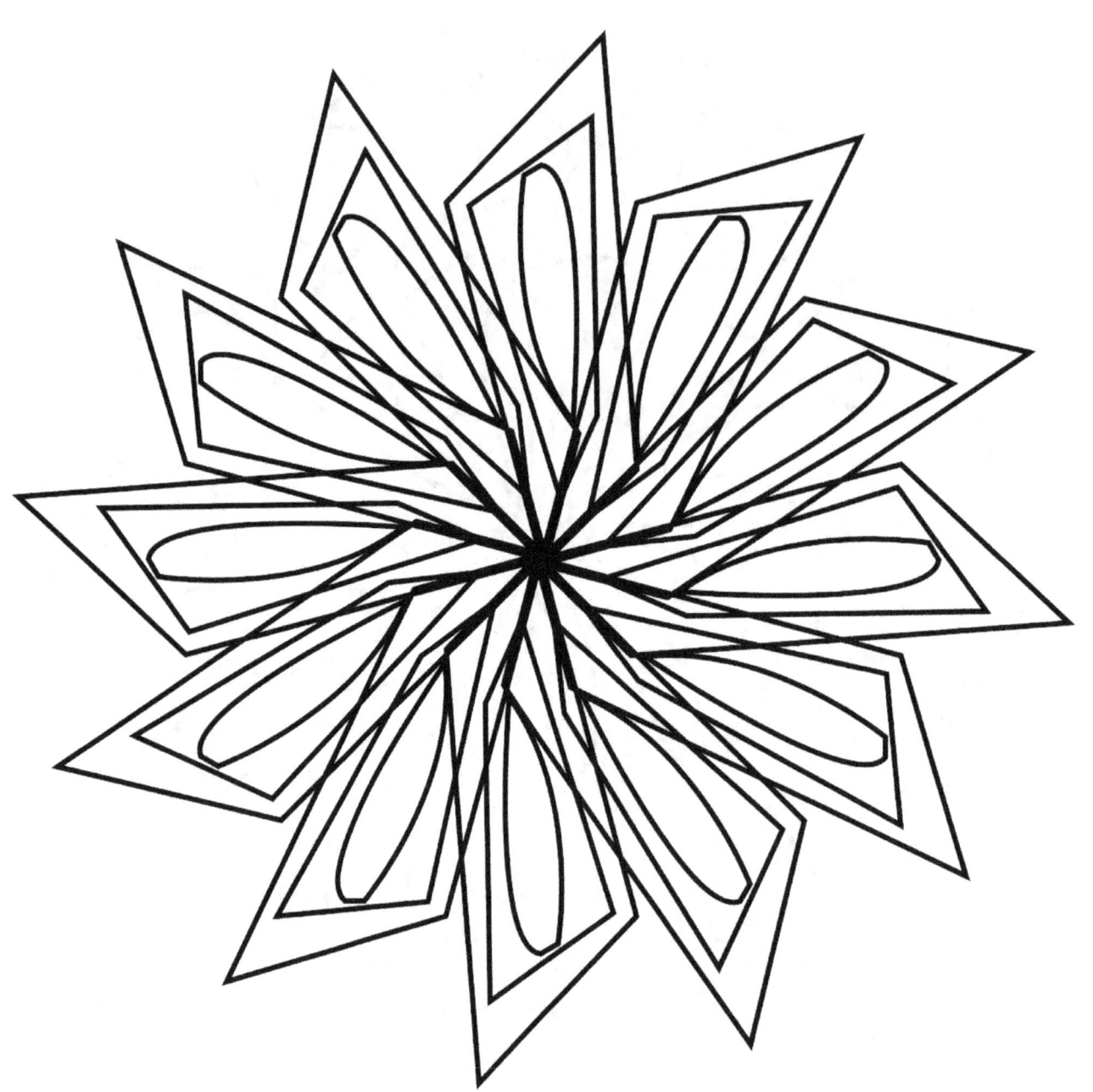

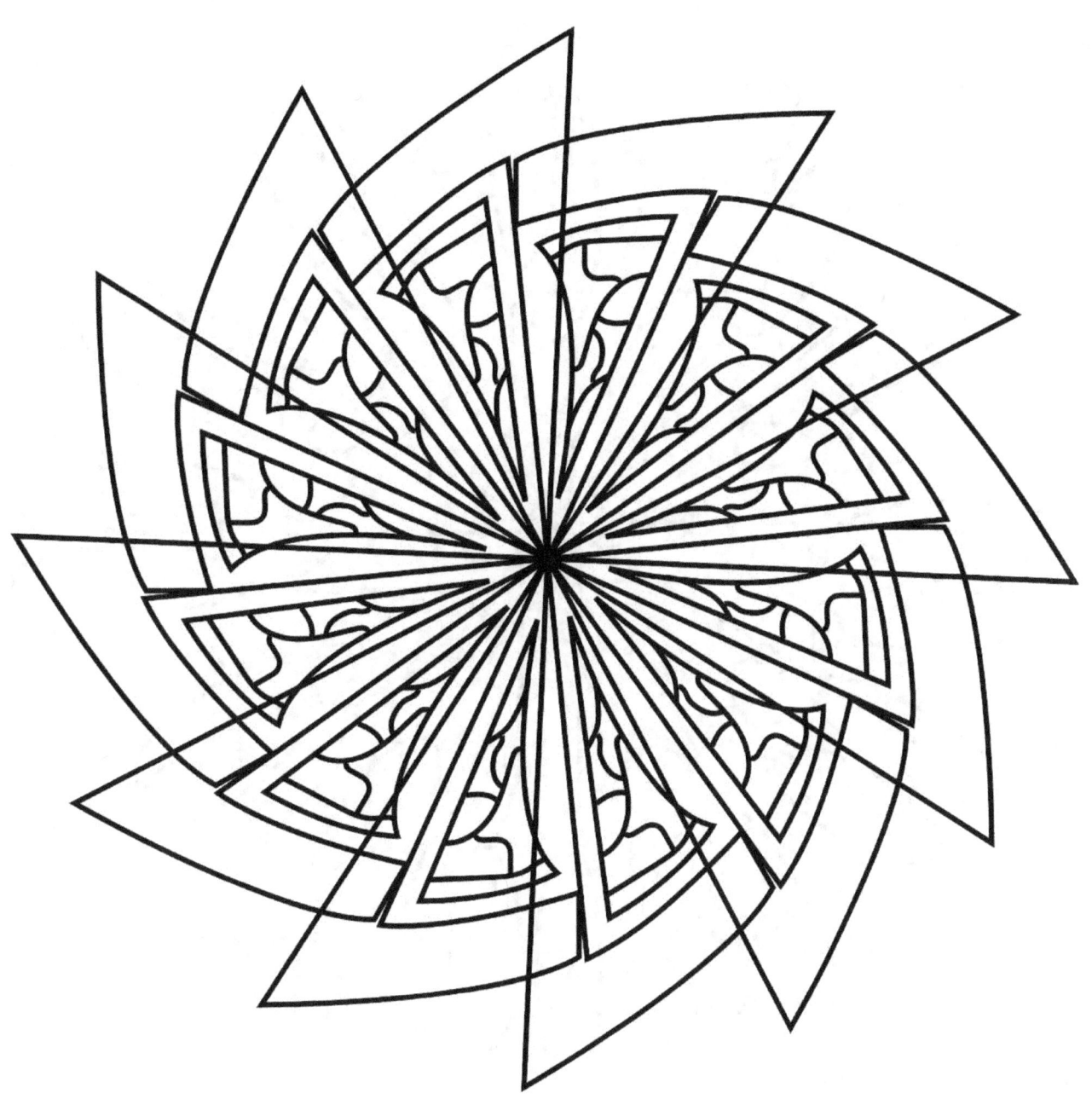

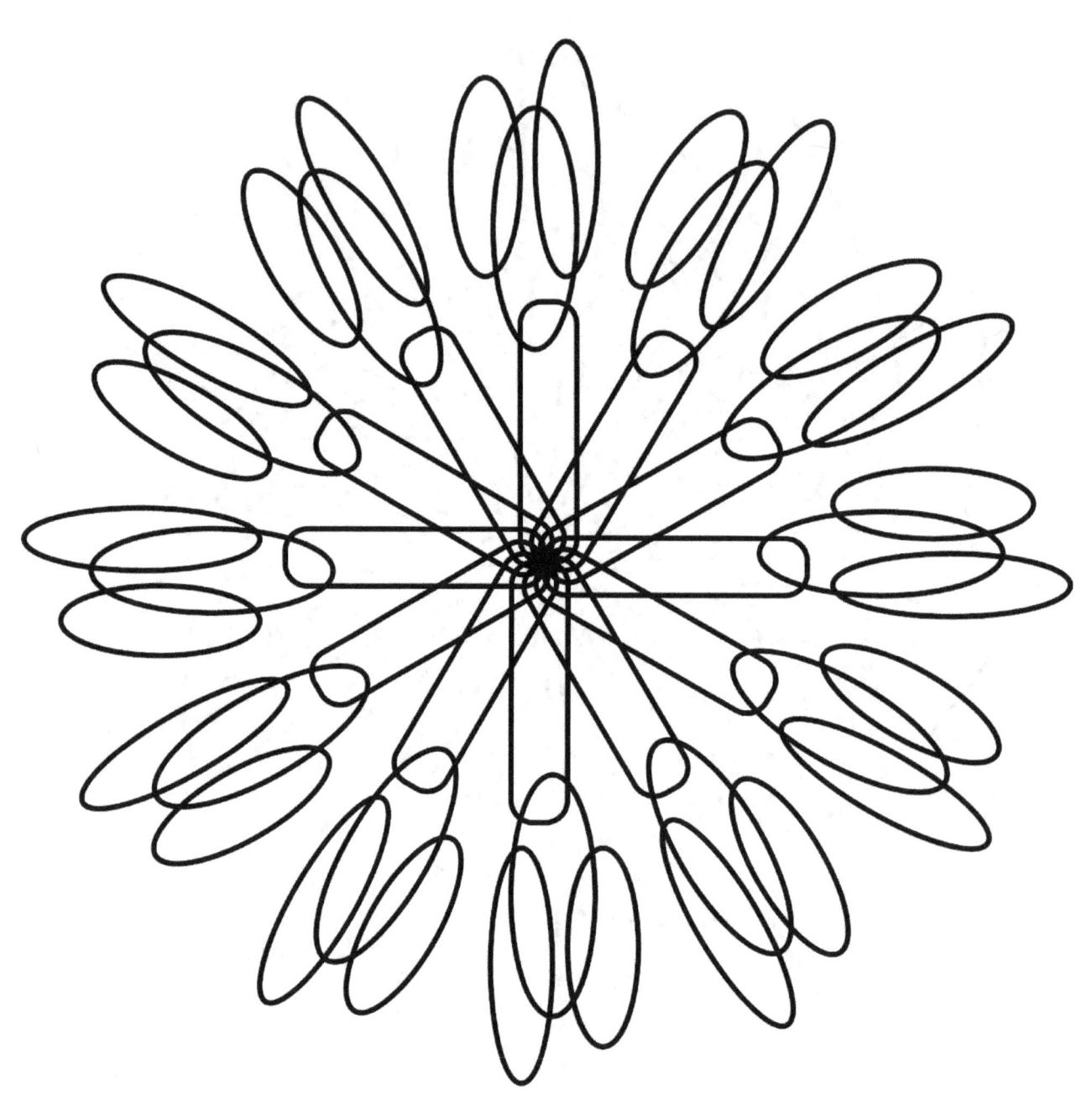

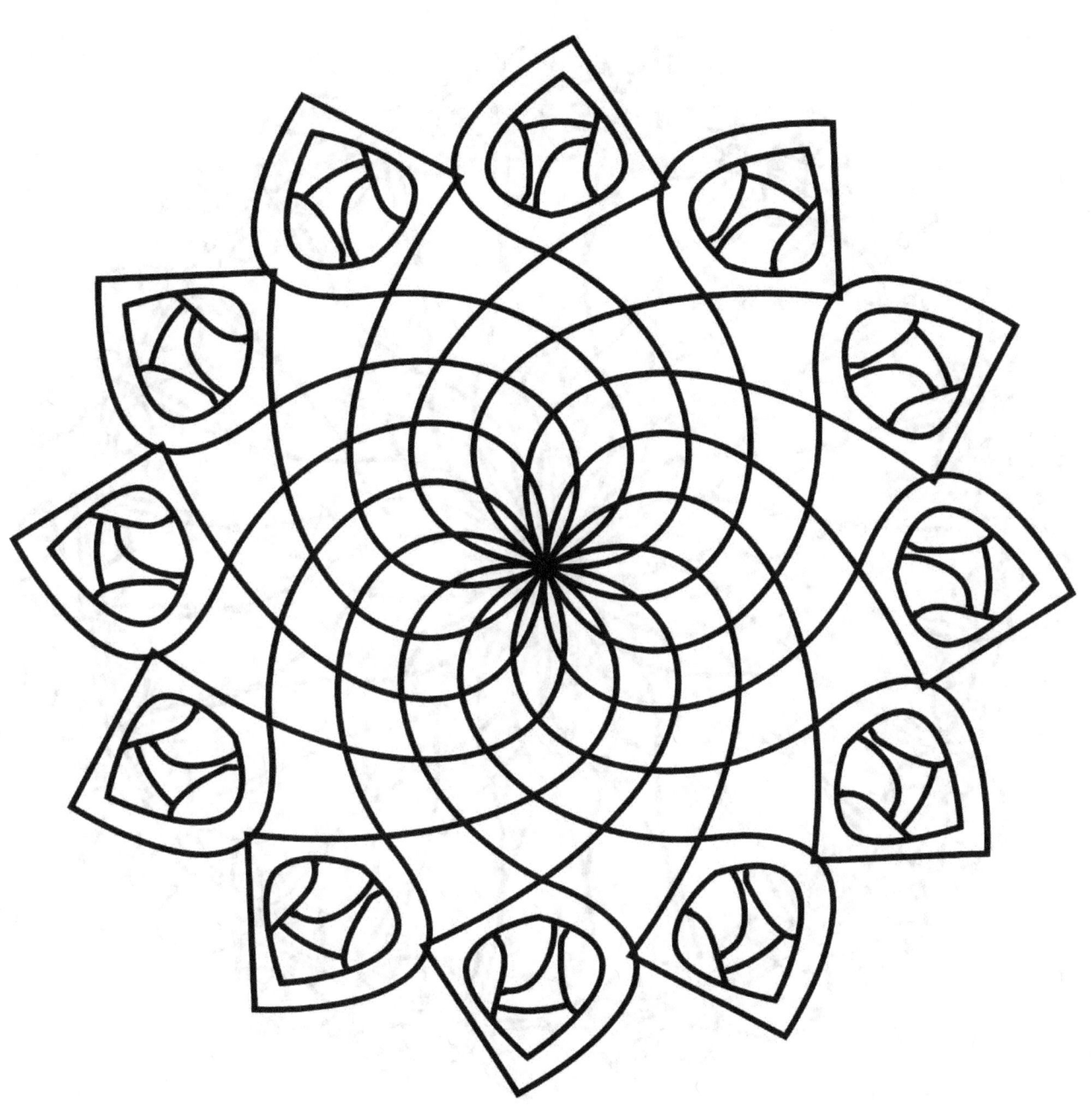

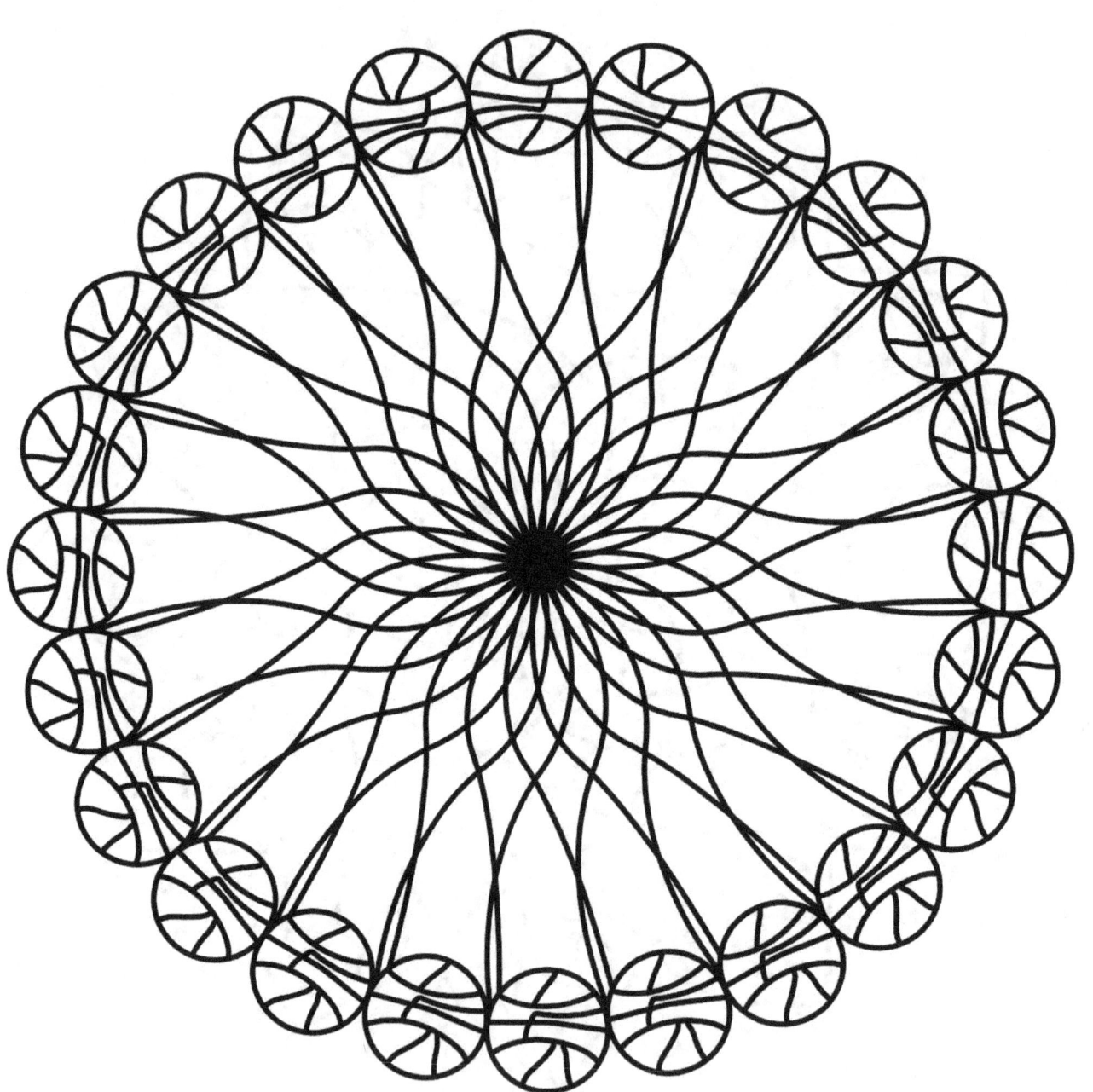

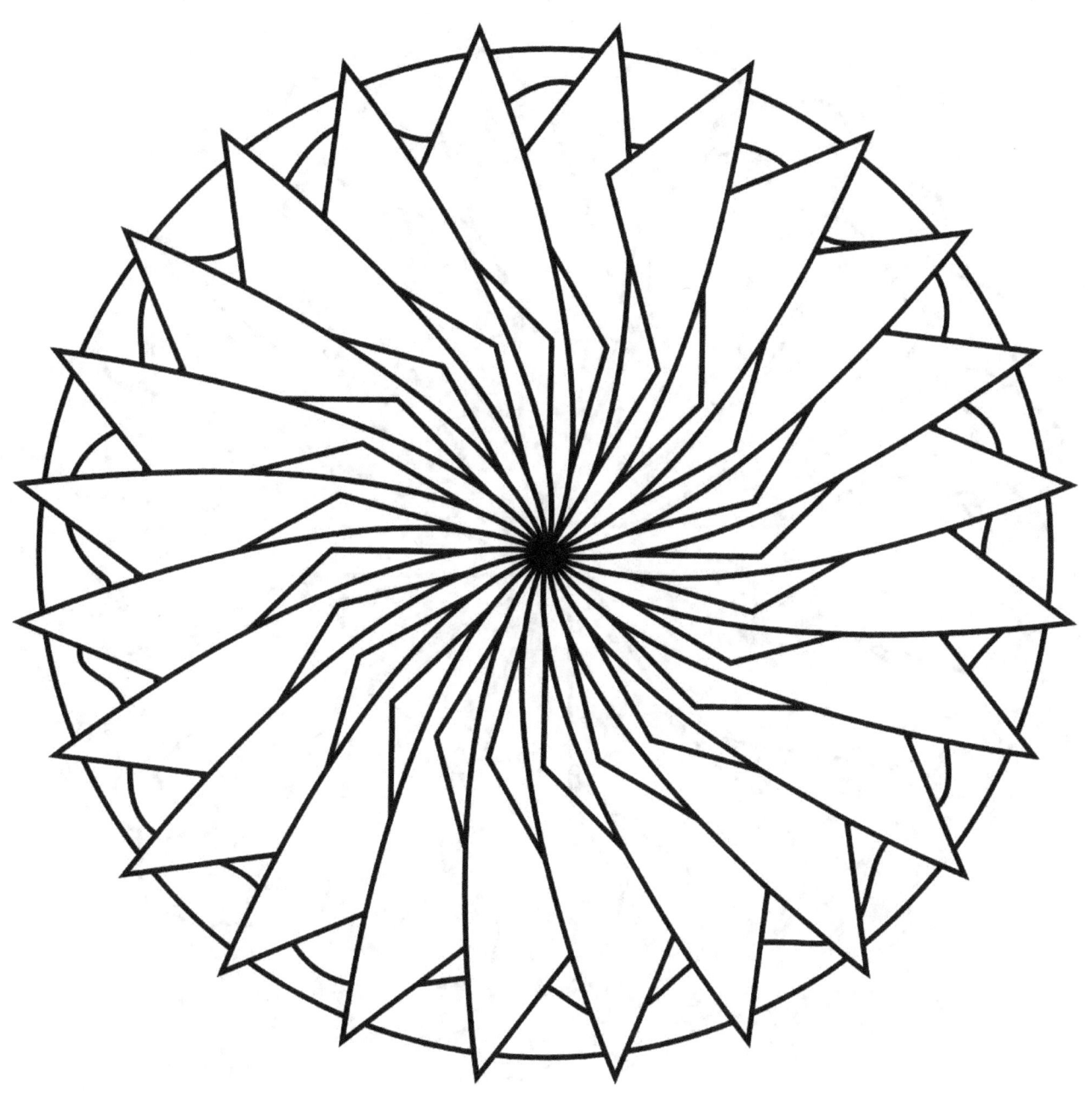

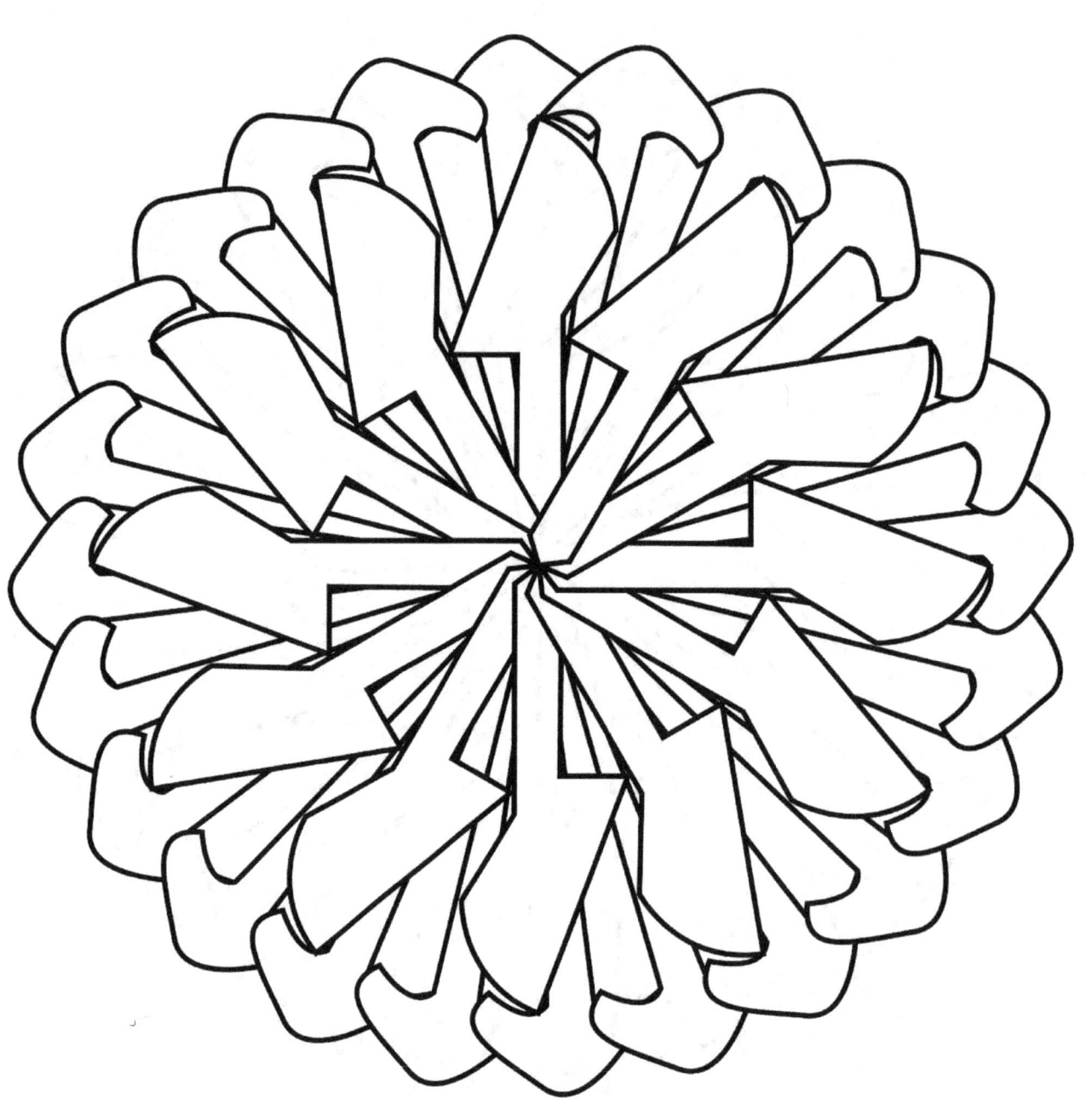

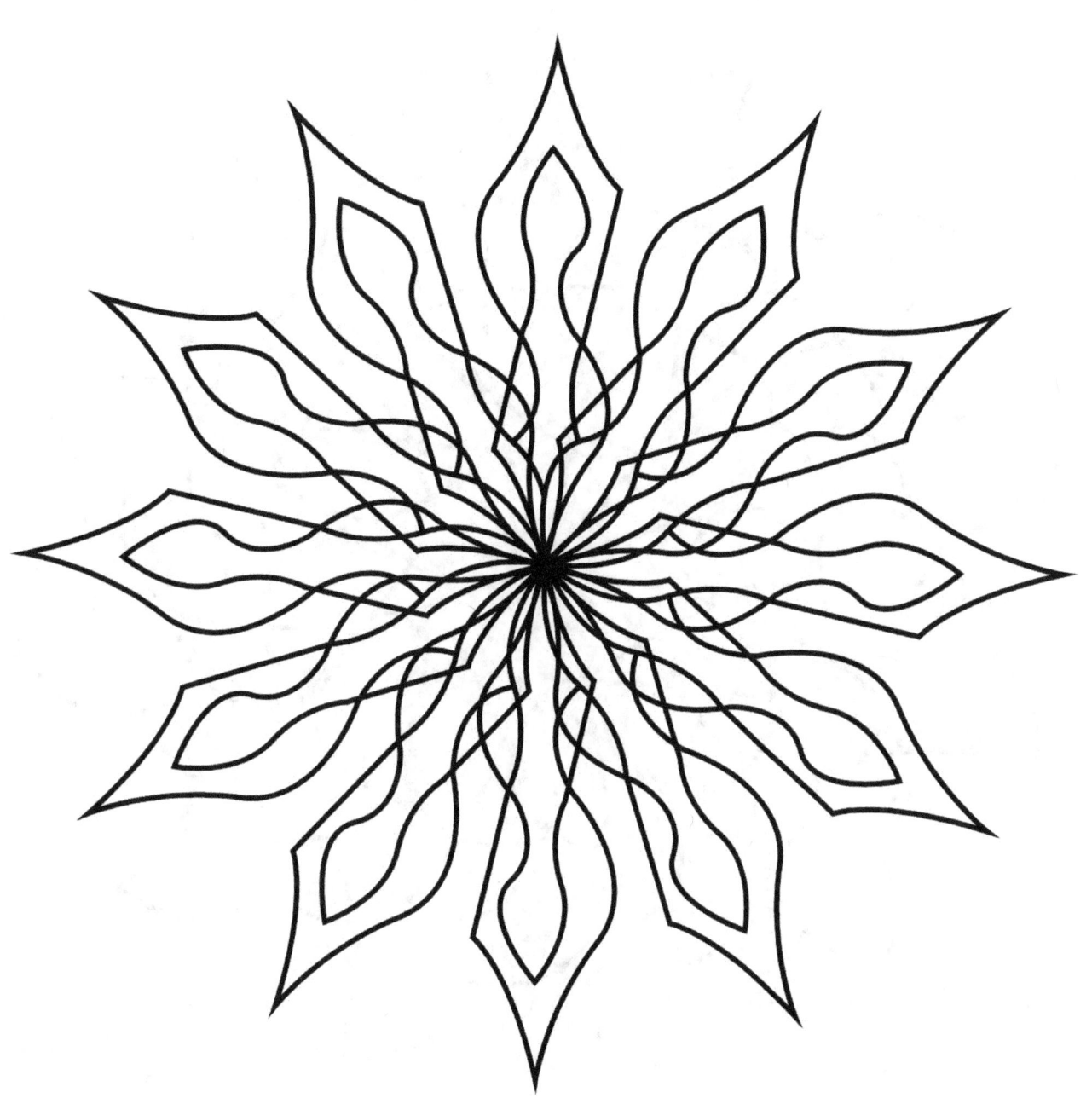

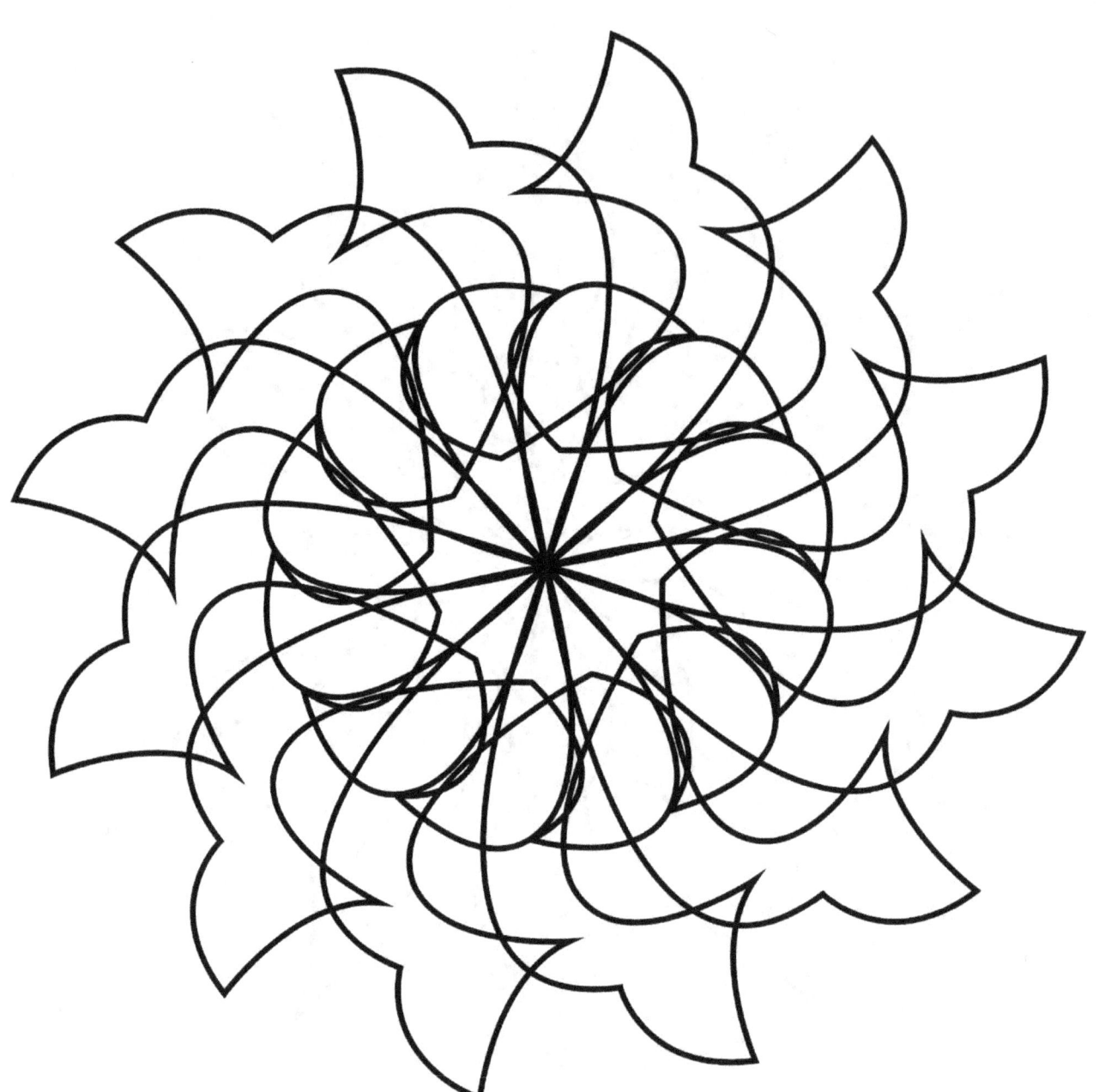

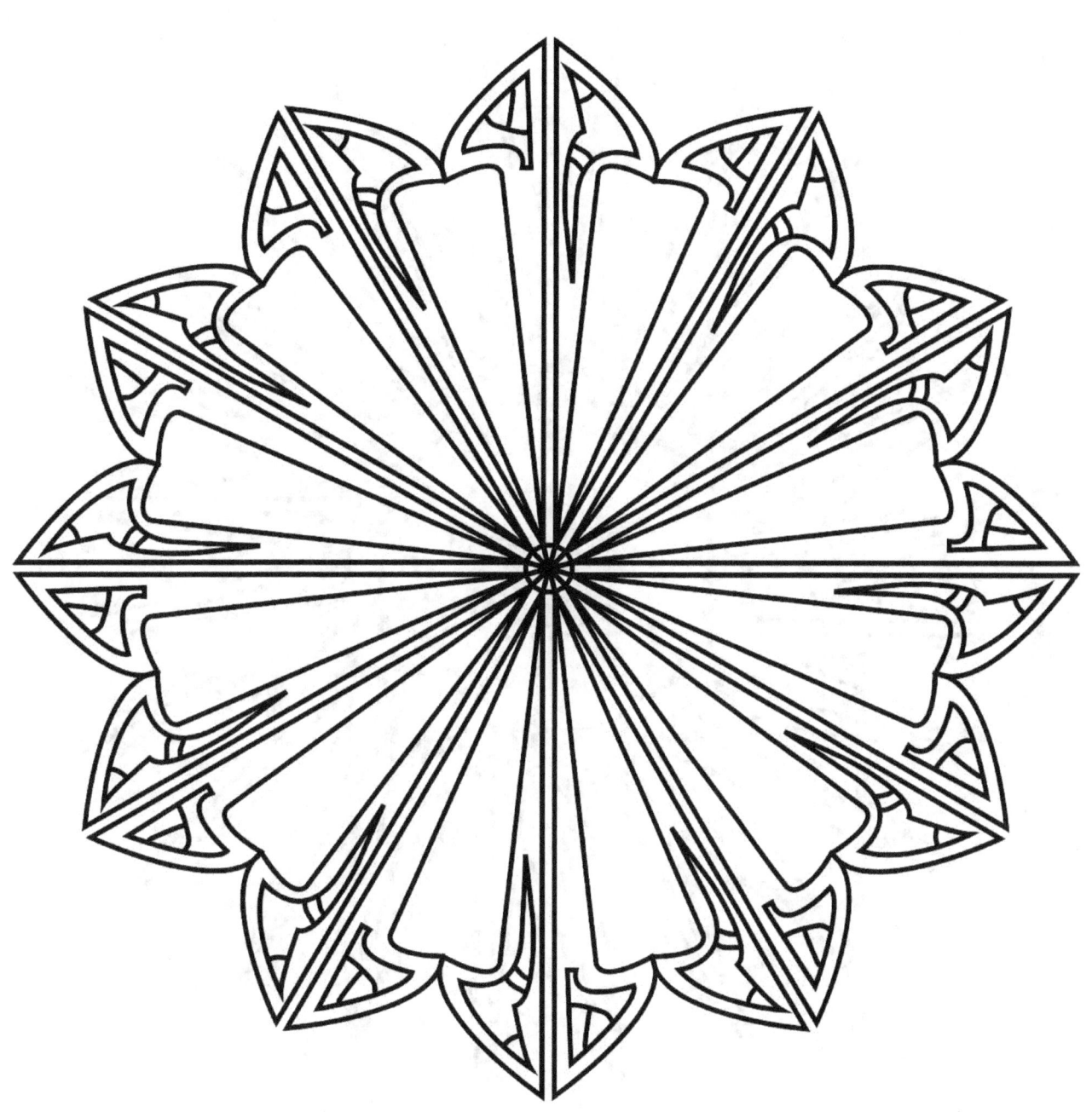

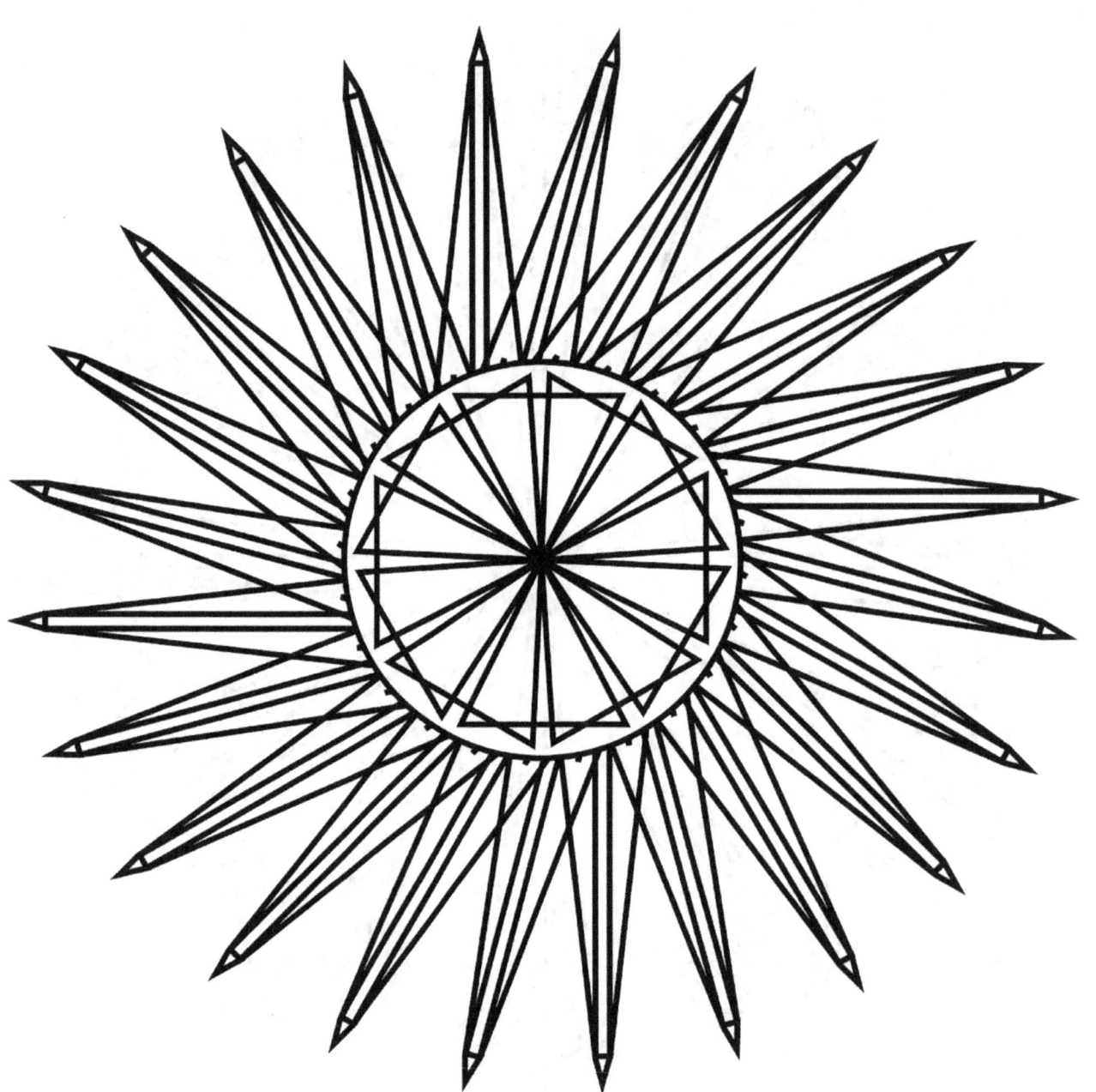

Thank you for choosing my humble book. I hope that you will enjoy coloring all of the illustrations within.

-----ENJOY-----